Talk & Toddle

A COMMONSENSE GUIDE
FOR THE FIRST THREE YEARS

Anne Marie Mueser, ED.D., coauthor of
While Waiting and *Welcome Baby*
Lynne M. Liptay, M.D., F.A.A.P.

ST. MARTIN'S PRESS / NEW YORK

Acknowledgments

Many people help make a book like *Talk & Toddle* become a reality. The authors would especially like to thank:

- Barbara Anderson, our editor, and Nina Barrett, her assistant, for doing their job so well, and for their never-ending encouragement; Harry Chester and his staff, for their high quality work (as always) and for their patience; Brandy Young of TypeCast, Inc., for reading as she set the type and for trying some of the material with her son; John Frost, for doing "just one more picture" several times; Brent Collins, Andrea Mueser, and Christine Tartaglia, for proofreading and help when needed most.

- The late Herb Birch, M.D., whose lectures and seminars in child development more than a decade ago, remain vividly in the mind of a former student.

- Pat Miskell and all our friends at Aer Lingus and Taylor Travel, who make traveling with a toddler pleasant as well as possible; Dr. Moriarty of the National Poison Control Network for his cooperation and the picture of *Mr. Yuk.*

- John Liptay, for his patience, helpful suggestions, careful proofreading, and photography; and Tommy, age 6, and Steven, age 3, who actively participated in their mother's publishing venture.

- Ánna Máire and her father, whose contributions are beyond measure or words; and her grandparents, whose love and childrearing talents made completion of *Talk & Toddle* possible at last.

Illustrated by John Frost
Edited by Barbara Anderson
Designed by Harry Chester Associates

Library of Congress Cataloging in Publication Data

Mueser, Anne Marie.
  Talk & toddle.

  1. Child rearing. 2. Infants. 3. Parent and child.
I. Liptay, Lynne M. II. Title. III. Title: Talk and toddle.
HQ769.M9255 1983   649'.122   83-3223
ISBN 0-312-78430-9 (pbk.)

First Edition

10 9 8 7 6 5 4 3 2 1

INTRODUCTION

When my daughter Ánna Máire was born, her arrival brought great joy which was immediately joined by the realization that there was much for me to learn. My early experiences as a new mother led to the book *Welcome Baby: A Guide to the First Six Weeks,* which contained many of the things I wish I had known sooner. Just about the time the research for *Welcome Baby* was completed, and I felt somewhat comfortable about taking care of a baby, Ánna Máire was well on her way into toddlerhood and it was time for another book. *Talk & Toddle: A Commonsense Guide for the First Three Years* is the inevitable sequel to *Welcome Baby.*

Dr. Liptay, the coauthor of *Talk & Toddle*, is a practicing pediatrician as well as the mother of two young children. Her experience as a physician has helped us to identify the topics of concern to today's parents and the questions most frequently asked. The content of *Talk & Toddle* is, of course, firmly based on research and our work as practicing professionals. Perhaps even more important, however, is the fact that we are both, right now, mothers of preschool children, and while writing this book we have had daily occasion to test our suggestions in the real world of our own lives. (The section on tantrums, for example, was written while Ánna Máire was busy having one because her mother wouldn't let her use the typewriter.) We feel that the immediacy of our experience—both personal and professional—gives *Talk & Toddle* an extra dash of authenticity and practicality.

Common sense is one of the most important ingredients of caring for a child. Don't be afraid to follow your own instincts, particularly when you have information to back them up. We hope *Talk & Toddle* will provide some of the information you need. Use this book as you work with your child's pediatrician, who may help you modify some of the suggestions as necessary to meet your child's special needs.

You'll notice that unlike some other childcare books, we don't have a special section addressed to the child's father. This is deliberate. All the material in *Talk & Toddle* (with the obvious exception of Weaning From the Breast) is intended for *both* parents. We hope you'll share the pleasures and tasks of parenting in whatever ways suit you best.

Anne Mueser, Ed.D.

Publisher's Note

The suggestions, procedures, and other materials in this book are not intended as a substitute for consultation with your physician. Medical supervision is recommended for care of your child and any other matters concerning your family's health.

Anne Marie Mueser, Ed.D., M.F.H.

Anne Marie Mueser, a writer and teacher for more than 15 years, has worked in elementary schools as a classroom teacher and reading specialist, and in clinical settings with learning disabled and dyslexic children. Formerly an Associate Professor of Education at Teachers College, Columbia University, Dr Mueser left the university in 1978 to devote her professional energies to her career as a writer. She is the author of numerous children's books and educational materials.

Dr. Mueser's first child, Ánna Máire, was born in August of 1980. She and her daughter divide their time between their homes in Dutchess County, New York, and County Galway, Ireland, where Dr. Mueser is a Joint Master of the Bermingham and North Galway Foxhounds.

Lynne M. Liptay, M.D., F.A.A.P.

Lynne M. Liptay is a pediatrician in private practice in Hyde Park, New York. She is on the staff of Northern Dutchess Hospital in Rhinebeck. Dr. Liptay received her M.D. degree from Yale University Medical School, and is a Fellow of the American Academy of Pediatrics.

Dr. Liptay lives with her family in Dutchess County, New York, where her husband John is an Electrical Engineer with IBM. The Liptays have two sons, Tom and Steven.

On the Cover

Ánna Máire was 19 months old when her uncle, John Mueser, took the cover picture for *Talk & Toddle.* Told to stand still for the picture, Ánna Máire, in typical toddler fashion, rolled once in the leaves before complying.

(L to R) The authors, Anne Mueser and Lynne Liptay, and their children Ánna Máire Mueser age 2½, Steven Liptay, age 3, and Tommy Liptay, age 6. (Photo by John Liptay)

TABLE OF CONTENTS

TALK & TODDLE

The arrival of a new baby, even if it's not your first, is likely to bring many changes to your household. Many of the caretaking techniques you work out in the early days, however, will become comfortable routines as you and your baby become more settled. Then, as the weeks turn into months, your infant will begin to become independently mobile, which will open up new worlds of excitement (and danger).

> For material on care of a very young baby, see *Wecome Baby: A Guide to the First Six Weeks*, by Anne Marie Mueser, Ed.D. and George Verrilli, M.D. (St. Martin's Press, New York: 1982). Although especially intended for parents of newborns, this book contains a number of suggestions which may be useful through the first few months, until it's time for *Talk & Toddle*.

You will have to cope with a certain amount of conflict as your child — no longer an infant in arms — becomes a toddler and strives for independence and mastery over the various tasks of living. The toddler phase, which for most children occurs approximately between ages one and three, is one of the most interesting developmental periods and also one of the most difficult — both for the child and for caregivers. The specific suggestions in *Talk & Toddle* are designed to help you encourage your child in development of self-control and autonomy, while at the same time providing appropriate limits and a safe environment.

> An excellent book to give you useful background information and insights about the dynamics of living with a toddler is *Toddlers and Parents: A Declaration of Independence*, by T. Berry Brazelton, M.D. (Dell Publishing Co., Inc., New York: 1974). The children described in this volume are carefully chosen examples of typical toddler behavior, and the reassuring way Dr. Brazelton describes how their parents can cope should give you courage and support.

According to the dictionary, the word toddle means "to go with short, unsteady steps." As your child grows, learns, struggles for independence, and the inevitable conflicts occur, there may be days you wonder which one of you is doing the toddling. Your toddler will surprise you with a series of new accomplishments, many of which will make new demands on your parenting skills. Don't be discouraged, and keep in mind that in most cases it's best to follow your instincts, even if you feel that your steps are a bit unsteady at first. The material in the pages that follow will provide information on many topics to help you take steps as a caregiver which are stronger, steadier, and more rewarding for you and your child.

Books on Child Care

During a visit to your local bookshop, you'd probably find many different books on topics concerning babies and children and their care. Some of these titles have been around for many years and have achieved considerable popularity among parents. For example, during the more than 35 years since the initial publication of *Baby and Child Care,* by Dr. Benjamin Spock (Simon & Schuster, New York: 1977), many millions of parents and other caregivers have consulted Dr. Spock's book for advice on medical and practical aspects of childrearing. Although some would disagree with certain of Dr. Spock's specific suggestions, many parents find the book to be a valuable resource. Another helpful title with a long history of previous printings and parental acceptance is *The Better Homes & Gardens New Baby Book* (Bantam Books, New York: 1980).

> An outstanding and comprehensive volume on baby and child care is *Your Baby & Child: From Birth to Age Five*, by Penelope Leach (Alfred A. Knopf, New York: 1981). This beautifully written book contains helpful information on all aspects of childcare. The author places special emphasis on sensitivity to the child's point of view and needs. Beautiful drawings and photographs — some of them in color — add to the book's appeal as an informative and caring work about young children.

For useful background information on the psychological development of young children, try reading *The Magic Years: Understanding and Handling the Problems of Early Childhood,* by Selma H. Fraiberg (Charles Scribner's Sons, New York: 1959). *The First Three Years of Life,* by Burton L. White (Avon Books, New York: 1975) is another title which many parents find worthwhile.

Many parents enjoy keeping track of important milestones in their child's development. To make it easy for you to do so, we have included the following chart. Already listed are milestones that occur during every child's first three years or so. The blank spaces are for you to list any special events or experiences that you wish to remember for your child.

MILESTONES AND MEMORIES

	Date	Notes
Says first word		
Says next words		
Sits alone		
Stands, holding on		
Plays peek-a-boo		
Feeds self (more or less)		
Creeps		
Waves bye-bye		
Walks, holding on		
Walks alone		

MILESTONES AND MEMORIES

	Date	Notes
Tries to undress self		
Goes up stairs		
Says "no"		
Scribbles		
Has tantrum		
Knows own name		
Dresses self (more or less)		
Names objects in pictures		
Turns pages		
Reads word or symbol		

Talk and Toddle from A to Z

Many child-care books are arranged chronologically, with different sections for the various ages and stages of a child's development. Although different children may differ greatly in the specific time they achieve certain developmental milestones, the sequence is generally the same for all. Chronological arrangement of information is especially appropriate for those whose children are typical. It may be somewhat disconcerting, however, in cases where a child is speedier or slower than the norm.

For ease of use, we have arranged *Talk & Toddle* alphabetically by topic. We expect that you would consult each section as the need arises with *your* child, not when someone else's list says it's time for you to encounter that particular problem or situation. Within a section, there may be different suggestions for a mobile baby (prewalking child) and toddler, if necessary.

The suggestions in *Talk & Toddle* are simply suggestions, not absolutes. Be sensitive to your child's responses and use what works best. We've tried to present the suggestions in plain, commonsense language and an easy-to-use format. We usually address you directly as *you,* rather than referring to you as "the primary caretaker," or some other impersonal term. Although it may occasionally result in an awkward sentence, we've tried to use both masculine and feminine pronouns at all times so that each suggestion will immediately apply to both boys and girls without the reader having to make that inference.

It may appear that an unusually large number of sections deal with accident prevention and what to do if the preventive measures have been less than successful. A toddler's energy and curiosity often exceed his or her judgment, and keeping the child safe is an important part of child care for this age. Troublesome behaviors such as dawdling, tantrums, excessive curiosity, and eating and sleeping problems, are all common to toddlerhood and receive considerable space. The toddler's struggle for independence does create numerous opportunities for conflict, but we don't want you to think that your child's toddler years are inevitably one problem after another. There are many exciting and wonderful times which emerge as your child grows. We hope that the suggestions in *Talk & Toddle* make it easier for you to nurture your child's development with a healthy minimum of conflict or unhappiness for either of you.

The pages that follow are an alphabetically arranged reference guide. The Table of Contents at the beginning of *Talk & Toddle*, and the Index on pages 152-153, can help you locate the topics you need quickly.

ACCIDENTS AND EMERGENCIES (First Aid)

Take a few minutes right now to plan how you would handle an emergency involving your mobile baby or toddler. You may never need to use these plans, but it's best to be ready just in case.

Know how to summon help fast when you need it. Look up the telephone numbers you might need in an emergency. Write them here and make a copy to keep by your telephone. Fasten the list securely to the wall or table by the phone so the numbers won't disappear just before you need one of them. Don't count on being able to remember anything in an emergency.

EMERGENCY TELEPHONE NUMBERS

Doctor_____

Hospital _____

Pharmacy _____

Rescue Squad or Ambulance _____

Police_____

Fire Department_____

Poison Control Center_____

Neighbor, Relative, or Friend_____

_____

_____

Make sure that baby-sitters or household employees know how to use these numbers if necessary.

If at all possible, you should take a course in CPR (Cardiopulmonary Resuscitation) and other first aid techniques. The techniques you learn may save someone's life. The first aid suggestions in this book may help give you some of the information you would need in an emergency, but it's best to learn directly from trained experts if you can.

The following sections of *Talk & Toddle* provide additional information about first aid procedures and how to respond to specific emergency situations. It's best to read these pages at least once before the need arises.

For additional material to help you deal with your child's medical problems — both illness and accidents — try *The Parents' Guide to Baby & Child Medical Care,* edited by Terril H. Hart, M.D. (Meadowbrook Press, Deephaven, MN: 1982). This handy guide provides lots of useful information in an easy-to-use format.

ACCIDENTS (Prevention)

It's up to you to provide as safe an environment for your child as possible. Many accidents to babies and toddlers occur at home, and many of them could have been prevented. Here are some things to keep in mind:

• Don't leave your mobile baby or toddler alone in a room. Take him or her with you to answer the phone or the door. If your child crawls or toddles out of sight, follow.

• Remember that your child is likely to imitate your actions. This can be very appealing for such behaviors as brushing the teeth or reading a magazine. It can be very dangerous if what the child attempts is lighting matches, taking pills, poking at fires, making tea, or plugging in and unplugging lamps or appliances.

• Beware of places that could trap your child. Wardrobes, closets, freezers, refrigerators, and similar containers can be death traps as well as hiding places. Be sure your child can't get locked in the bathroom or any other room of your home. A folded towel hung over the top of the bathroom door will keep a child from closing the door completely.

• Make sure there is nothing that your toddler can pull down from overhead. A tug on the corner of a tablecloth can pull the table's entire contents along with it. The cord of an iron, toaster, or food processor can bring the appliance crashing down on a small head.

• Keep all poisonous household materials such as detergent, cleaning fluid, deodorizers, furniture polish, and paint where your child can't get to them. This means completely out of reach. Don't count on childproof containers to do the job. Kitchen baseboard cabinets should have childproof latches or be completely cleared of dangerous materials.

• Make sure that any furniture your child might use to pull himself or herself up is sturdy enough to support an active toddler and secure enough not to tip over.

• Watch out for sharp edges and corners at your child's face level.

• Your medicine cabinet should be locked. Discard any substances not in current use. Don't refer to medicine (even vitamins) as candy. Be careful not to leave items you use routinely (e.g., oral contraceptives, vitamins, and aspirin) where your child can get to them.

• A mother's handbag is an enticing object. Don't keep anything in it that your toddler shouldn't get to. If you must carry medication with you, take only a day's supply at a time, and don't leave your purse where your child can freely explore.

• Prevent choking. Don't leave your child alone with a bottle or food. Keep items small enough to choke a child (marbles, coins, buttons, etc.) out of reach. Don't serve a toddler a drink in a styrofoam cup because it could easily be bitten into small pieces.

• Prevent suffocation. Keep plastic bags or food wrap away from children. Don't use thin plastic as a mattress cover. A small child should not use a pillow in the crib.

• A young child can drown in as little as two inches of water. Never leave your baby or toddler unsupervised in the bath or near a body of water (whether it be a deep puddle or a swimming pool).

• A bathroom is not a safe place for a mobile baby or toddler to be for even a few moments without supervision. The surfaces are hard and slippery. A dive into an empty tub (or one with water) could cause serious injury. A toddler's fascination with the toilet can be hazardous to valued objects and the plumbing as well as to the child. Although unlikely, it is possible for a young child to fall head first into the toilet bowl and to drown. This has been known to happen. Keep the toilet lid down and the bathroom door shut.

• Unused electric outlets should be capped so that your child can't poke things into them. Keep your child away from outlets that are in use. If these outlets can be made inaccessible by large pieces of furniture, so much the better.

• Automatic garage doors can be very dangerous. If you have one, always make sure your child is safe and under your control before you close it. Don't leave the transmitter where a child could get to it. Children have been known to crush themselves while playing with the controls of automatic doors.

• Windows should have guards to prevent falls. Don't assume that your child will be unable to open a window or will be obedient enough to stay away from one. Make sure the window guards are strong and properly installed.

• Space heaters can cause serious burns as well as fires if tipped over. Keep any portable heaters and children well apart.

• Prevent scalding. If your hot water temperature is hot enough to cause a problem, either adjust the setting or make sure that your child does not have access to the taps at any time. Be careful of the teakettle or coffeepot. Don't set hot liquid on a surface or cloth within reach of a child.

• Appliances such as blenders, food processors, mixers, or fans should be left unplugged and out of reach. Keep tools, garden equipment, and sharp kitchen implements away from a small child.

• Your house is likely to contain many substances that aren't obviously poisonous but which could, if consumed in quantity, seriously injure your child. Among these are many cosmetics, alcoholic beverages, and a number of innocent-looking house plants. (See also Poisoning, page 105.) Ask your local Poison Control Center how you can obtain the Public Information Bulletin identifying 50 common harmful plants.

• Beware of anything that could get caught around a child's neck. This includes drapery and venetian blind cords, clothesline, and the cord of your telephone. Items such as these should not be within reach of a child's crib.

• Keeping objects out of reach isn't always so easy. Out of reach means that a child can't pile things and climb to the forbidden objects. Some children seem to be natural climbers and explorers. If your child is one of these, you'll have to be extra careful. Remove not only the dangerous objects, but also the means to get to them.

• No matter how carefully you have arranged your *own* living quarters for your child's safety, remember that your friends and relatives are unlikely to have done the same. Be especially attentive to your mobile baby or toddler when you are visiting. A good rule to remember at home or away is, "A toddler out of sight (unless sleeping soundly) is a child at risk."

For additional specific suggestions on preventing accidents at home, see Childproofing, page 40; Fire, page 73; Safety Gates, page 109; and Safety Harnesses, page 110. To keep your child safe in an automobile, see Automobile Safety, page 15.

ADOPTED CHILDREN

The needs of an adopted child are the same as those of any other child: love, security, and feelings of belonging, as well as food, clothing, and shelter.

It is generally agreed that an adopted child should be told that he or she is adopted. The best time and way to do this is whenever it is natural and comfortable for you to do so. Answer your child's questions, and don't tell lies you'll have to undo later. On the other hand, don't volunteer more information than the child requires or is able to handle. While you shouldn't avoid the issue, don't go overboard in talking about adoption with a young child either. If you keep bringing the topic up, the child may get the idea that you are uncomfortable with it. The best way to make any child—adopted or not—feel secure, is to provide a loving, supportive, and predictable environment.

AGGRESSIVE BEHAVIOR

Some aggressive behavior is normal for a toddler who is actively engaged in acquiring independence. A toddler lacks the understanding and the social controls to manage aggressive behavior, and adult intervention is often required to keep characteristic toddler assertiveness from getting out of hand. Helping a toddler to become a civilized human being takes tact, energy, and lots of patience.

A toddler may well treat other children as things rather than as persons, and grab for them or push them aside as the whim strikes. This is normal, and children can be permitted to work these things out for themselves as long as no one gets hurt. If one toddler, for example, grabs a toy and the other says, "NO!" and takes the toy back, this exchange will cause no harm and may even be a beginning step toward learning to share. If, however, a child bites or kicks, hits or pushes hard, or uses toys as clubs or missiles, then you must intervene immediately. Stop the toddler from whatever it is he or she should not be doing. Firmly say, "No, you must not (kick, bite, hit, etc.)." You may at the same time have to protect and comfort the victim. You might try picking up the child who needs protection in one arm and using the other to restrain the child who's out of control. Do whatever seems to make the most sense. Do it quietly and firmly. Don't scream or hit. If you combat your child's aggression with more of the

same, you may indeed end the immediate crisis. However, clobbering a toddler will do more to set a bad example than to teach self control and socially acceptable behavior.

Should you encourage your child to stand up for his or her rights by fighting back if another child becomes aggressive? It's fine to let children try to settle minor disputes through give and take. It's not fine to encourage violence and to permit a child to hurt someone else. Toddlers are not yet able to think through the social consequences of their behavior, so you or another caregiving adult will have to draw the line between healthy assertiveness and unacceptable aggression. (See also Biting, page 28.)

ALCOHOLIC BEVERAGES

Is it all right to give a small child a sip of wine or beer or a taste of a cocktail? Opinions vary. Some pediatricians and psychologists would answer a firm "No" to this question and advise against introducing a child to the taste of alcohol for any reason. Others would say that an occasional sip of a parent's drink causes no harm and avoids giving drink the special appeal of forbidden fruit. Whichever approach suits your family, we suggest that you follow it without making a fuss one way or the other. Here are some additional guidelines.

• If your family has wine at dinner or for special occasions and rituals, and you wish to permit your young child to be part of that experience, a few drops of wine in a cordial glass filled with water will do very nicely.

• If one parent has strong feelings against drinking for any reason, it's best for both parents to respect those feelings and not let giving the child an occasional sip become a source of conflict. One parent should not let the child take a swallow if doing so upsets or offends the other parent. Both parents should agree on the approach to alcohol they are going to take, and not argue about it in front of the child.

• No matter what your views on an occasional sip for your child, alcoholic beverages should be stored out of your child's reach. A very big drink in a very small person has been known to cause serious harm, even death.

11

• Don't leave the remnants of last night's party where your child can finish off the drinks your guests didn't. More than one parent has come into the living room the next morning to find a tipsy toddler who rose early and had another party.

Remember that alcohol is a drug and no child needs it. An *occasional* swallow is unlikely to do your child any physical harm. Some physicians even recommend rubbing brandy or whisky on the gums to relieve teething pain. Use your own judgment. The best rule to follow is common sense.

ALLERGIES

A tendency to allergic reactions often runs in families, although a child's allergies may take an entirely different form from those of a parent. What are allergies and why do some people have them? The environment is full of substances that cause little or no bother to most people, although some substances are potentially harmful. The body of a person with allergies has an abnormally sensitive reaction to one or more substances that for most people would cause no harm.

There are four main categories of substances which can trigger allergic reactions. They are divided according to the way a person comes in contact with them:

(1) things that are swallowed (foods, drinks, medicines)
(2) things that are breathed (dust, pollen, feathers, animal dander, etc.)
(3) things that are touched (dyes, poisonous plants, wool, plastic, detergents, etc.)
(4) things that are injected (medications, venom from bites)

Things that Are Swallowed (Foods, Drinks, Medicines)

A high percentage of allergic reactions in babies and toddlers involves food. A child's sensitivity to food substances may result in digestive problems, breathing difficulties (asthma), or skin rashes (eczema or hives). In a bottle-fed infant, allergy to cow's milk formula may develop. If so, a soybean-based formula is often prescribed as a substitute.

If allergic reactions tend to run in your family, you should be careful about the introduction of new foods to your baby. Certain foods are known to be more likely to cause a problem than others, and it's wise to be aware of what these foods are so you can be especially cautious about them and delay using them if you suspect a possible problem. Among the most common allergy-provoking foods are products containing wheat (gluten), eggs, citrus fruits, strawberries, chocolate, peanuts, tomatoes, corn, artificial food colorings, and cow's milk.

To identify possible food problems, it's best to introduce new foods one at a time and in very small quantities to your baby. Begin with a tiny portion—a teaspoonful or less—and feed the new food as part of the diet for at least a week. If no reaction occurs, then you can introduce something else. If you present more than one new food at a time and an allergic reaction does occur, you won't be able to identify the offending item.

If you suspect that your child is experiencing any food allergies, it's best to work with your doctor in identifying the problem.

Many children become less sensitive to certain foods as they grow older, and it may be possible to avoid triggering an allergic reaction by waiting a while before offering a food that might cause trouble. For example, some infants under six months of age are sensitive to eggs, and feeding them eggs would set off allergic reactions. Many of these same children, however, would have no problem with eggs if they didn't have their first egg until after their first birthday.

Things that Are Breathed (Dust, Pollen, Feathers, Animal Dander, Etc.)

There are many things around us which, if breathed, can cause an allergic reaction in a sensitive person. Among these are household dust, animal dander (the scaly stuff that flakes off an animal's skin at the base of the hair), pollen, feathers, and smoke.

Wheezing, sneezing, runny noses, and in severe cases asthma, are often a result of allergy to something breathed. If you suspect that your child has an allergy that is causing any or all of these symptoms, consult your physician.

If dust is the problem, you'll probably have to be extra meticulous about cleaning the house. You'll have to keep the child's room as free of dust as possible. This may involve getting rid of the rug, drapes, curtains, and any other surfaces which hold the dust. Use a wet mop or cloth on all the surfaces daily. Eliminate dusty toys (fluffy stuffed animals) for a while.

If you suspect that a household pet is the source of the difficulty, begin by keeping the animal away from direct contact with your child. Keep the pet out of rooms where your child crawls, walks, or spends any significant period of time. Use the vacuum cleaner at least once a day to remove animal hair and dander from the rugs and furniture. Your veterinarian may prescribe a spray to use on the animal to reduce the amount of loose dander that is shed. If the animal is an important part of your family, ask your pediatrician to recommend an allergist who works with children. Before you resort to giving your pet away, you should find out definitely if it is indeed the animal that's causing the problem. It would be very sad to give away the beloved family dog and then find out that the child's problem wasn't the dog, but feathers from the sofa pillows.

Things that Are Touched (Dyes, Plants, Wool, Plastic, Detergents, Etc.)

If your child seems prone to skin rashes, you might suspect a contact allergy of some sort. Try to figure out what substance regularly comes in contact with the affected part. For example, a rash around the waist and top of each leg would suggest the plastic from the edge of a disposable diaper or perhaps waterproof pants. A rash around the neck might be from the top of a wool sweater. A rash in various places under the clothing might be a reaction to detergent residues which remain in the clothes after laundering. Once you've identified the suspect, keep that substance away from your child's skin. If detergents are the problem, run the clothes through an extra rinse cycle to get out the residue.

Things that Are Injected (Medications, Venom from Bites)

Certain types of allergic reaction—to penicillin, or bee stings, for example—can be very serious, even life-threatening. You won't know for sure if your child has a problem until the first time an allergic reaction to an injected medication or a sting or bite occurs. If your child shows any signs of an allergic reaction to a substance which has been introduced into the body by injection or sting, call your physician immediately. Be especially alert for breathing difficulty, swelling, fever or rash.

ANTIBIOTICS

Antibiotics can be very useful and in some cases lifesaving drugs. However, you should not administer any such medication to your child without a doctor's prescription. Unnecessary use of antibiotics may sensitize a child and result in allergic reactions as well as help the body develop resistant strains of bacteria. This could cause a problem if the child later comes down with a serious illness that requires antibiotic treatment.

If your child becomes ill and the doctor prescribes antibiotics, follow the directions exactly. Use up *all* the medicine as directed, even if the pain, fever, or other symptoms have passed. Don't save any for next time. Even if your child appears better, the complete course of medication is probably needed to rid his or her system of the infection.

ASTHMA

Asthma is an allergic reaction in which the bronchial tubes become swollen and thick with mucus, causing a wheezing sound as the person tries to breathe. The muscle spasms that accompany an asthma attack make breathing (especially exhaling) extremely difficult, often resulting in panic which, in turn, only makes matters worse.

If your child has an apparent asthma attack for the first time, you should get immediate medical assistance. If possible, let someone else call the doctor while you help the child. Support the child in a sitting position. Be calm, reassuring, and comforting. Getting the child to relax will make it easier for him or her to breathe. Diversions such as a favorite story or record, or a quiet game may help. Adding moisture to the air (see Vaporizers, page 142) may be beneficial.

The doctor may prescribe medication for you to have on hand so that you can deal with any future asthma attacks as they occur. If you have been instructed on how to treat your child during an attack, it may not be necessary for you to summon medical aid each time. Your doctor will advise you on this.

If your child has a tendency toward asthma attacks, you will have to work closely with your doctor to identify and avoid the specific causes in your child's case. Feathers, animal hair, wool, and dust are among the most common triggers for these allergic reactions. Emotional factors (such as anxiety or tension) as well as environment may contribute to the severity of the attacks. In order to get the help you need to bring your child's attacks under control, it's important for you to be open and honest in your talks with your child's doctor. Don't be afraid or embarrassed to mention tensions or problems in the home if there are any. This information may be useful.

Some children seem to outgrow asthma attacks as they get older. Others do not. It's usually possible, however, to ease the problem so that it's not as upsetting.

AUTOMOBILE SAFETY

Automobile accidents are the leading cause of death and serious injury for children under the age of five. What makes this statistic especially shocking is that many—perhaps up to 90 per cent—of these automobile tragedies could be prevented if all car-travelling children were correctly secured in approved safety restraint systems. It makes no sense that many otherwise caring, careful, and conscientious parents so casually place their children in jeopardy every time they get into an automobile.

Why Use a Restraint System?

• A properly designed and correctly used restraint system can prevent serious injury and perhaps save your child's life in the event of an accident.

• Holding a child is no protection. An infant on an adult's lap could be crushed during a crash, or could be sent flying about the car with great force. Even a sharp stop could catapult and severely injure an unrestrained child.

• It needn't take a crash to kill a child with a car. Many children fall out of windows or doors. A car restraint prevents this.

• A restrained child cannot interfere with or distract the car's driver.

• In many states, carrying a child without an approved restraint system is now illegal as well as dangerous.

• Adult seatbelts are not suitable for young children. They may not restrain the child and in the event of a crash may even cause internal injuries.

Common Excuses

• "Using the restraint takes time." This is true, but it's time well spent. The currently available restraint systems are easier to use (as well as safer) than a number of the earlier models.

• "Car restraints are expensive." This is true, but surely your child's life is worth more than the price of the restraint. And, if getting together the necessary cash is a problem, it may be possible to rent or to borrow a car seat. Ask your doctor for suggestions. In many areas, civic groups such as the Chamber of Commerce have programs to help families acquire car restraints for their children.

• "My child doesn't like to be strapped in." A child who is *always* fastened correctly before the car is allowed to move will not mind the restraint. Such a child knows no other way to travel. Once you make an exception or two to this rule, you may be headed for trouble. Even so, this is a time when the child's wishes should not govern your actions. You wouldn't let your toddler jump off the roof or light a fire on the carpet. So, why would you consider letting the child dictate an unsafe practice in your automobile?

• "We're only going to the corner store." A very high percentage of accidents occur within a few miles of home. And, what might be an insignificant fender bender for an adult could cause serious injury or death to a small child.

• "I'm a good driver." No matter how true this is, there are a number of people on the road who are not. If someone hits you, the fact that you didn't cause the accident will be no comfort if your child is injured or killed. An animal crossing your path, a patch of ice, a sudden glare of sun in your eyes, or any one of many unpredictable things could cause a problem no matter how skilled a driver you might be.

Choosing a Car Restraint

It doesn't matter which car restraint you use for your child as long as the one you choose meets current safety standards and you put your child in it every time you take him or her out in an automobile. Federal specifications for car restraints were updated in 1981 to make the devices safer and easier to use.

Make sure that the restraint you choose fits in your car. If a permanent tether strap is required for the model you purchase, make sure to have it installed properly in your car. Be careful to select a car restraint that *you* find easy to use so that you're not tempted to skip using it.

> To find out more about infant and child car seats, get the pamphlet called "Don't Risk Your Child's Life," published by Physicians for Automotive Safety. Send 35¢ and a stamped, self-addressed envelope to *Physicians for Automotive Safety*, 50 Union Avenue, Irvington, N J 17111. It contains useful information about available products, along with brand names and model numbers of safe car seats. This pamphlet is revised frequently and is an excellent source of up-to-date information.

BABYFOOD (Commercially Prepared)

For many parents, the convenience of commercially prepared baby foods justifies the cost. If you prefer to purchase little jars instead of making your own baby food, go right ahead and don't feel guilty about it. Home cooking is very nice, but not an essential ingredient of good parenting. You can use commercially prepared baby foods to meet your baby's nutritional needs if you choose and purchase items carefully and pay attention to the labels. Here are some hints for using commercially prepared baby foods.

• Be sure the safety seal on each jar you buy has not been broken. If the little button on the top of the jar has already popped up, the jar isn't sealed and should be discarded. Check the expiration date before purchase or use.

• Read the list of ingredients and the nutritional information on the jar's label and choose carefully. The order in which ingredients are listed is important. What the jar contains most of is listed first. A jar with "carrots, potatoes, water, beef. . . ." contains less meat than the same size container labeled "beef, carrots, water. . . ." It's best to avoid products with modified starches or sugars added.

• Mixed dinners, which often contain fillers, are not as good a buy as plain meat or vegetables. If your baby doesn't like the texture of the plain strained meats, try mixing a spoon or two of meat with a vegetable, mashed potatoes, or one of the combinations.

• Unless you expect to feed the entire container at one meal, don't feed directly from the jar. Saliva and bacteria from your baby's mouth can speed up spoilage, and you risk making the child sick with a later meal from the same jar.

• If you heat the food, remember that warm, not hot, is suitable. Room temperature is fine too. Remove what you intend to use from the jar and heat only that. To be on the safe side, don't keep food that's already been heated.

• Opened jars should be stored in the refrigerator. Throw away any that have not been used by the end of the third day. (If you don't want to throw them out, put the remains in soup or feed them to the dog.) Open a fresh jar for the baby.

• Even if you find the food bland and boring, don't add salt to make it more appealing to your adult taste. Your baby doesn't need the extra sodium.

By the age of eight months or so, most babies are ready to handle the coarser consistency of junior foods. If your child is ready for junior foods, he or she will also be able to handle many items from the family table as long as you mash them up. However, if you find the jars convenient, there's no reason not to use them. Commercially prepared junior foods are safe and, if carefully selected, can provide your child with a nutritious diet. Many parents find a combination of commercially prepared and homemade foods to work best.

17

BABYFOOD (Homemade)

Homemade babyfood can be an economical and nutritious way to bridge the gap between the all-milk diet of an infant and the family table meals of an older toddler. Many families prefer to make their own babyfood instead of purchasing commercially prepared jars and packages.

Making your own babyfood doesn't require elaborate equipment. A pot with a tight fitting lid and a steamer basket are all you need to cook the food. (Steaming vegetables rather than boiling them in a lot of water helps to preserve the vitamins and other nutrients.) A blender or food processor will puree a portion of whatever family food you wish to serve your baby. If you don't have one of these appliances, don't go out and buy one just for your baby's sake. The mushy food stage doesn't last long enough to justify the cost. A hand operated food grinder (very inexpensive) will do the job nicely. Long before any of these devices were available, mothers mashed baby's dinner with a fork. It still works.

To make one meal at a time for baby, simply steam and mash or puree a small portion. Remove your baby's food from the pot before adding salt or highly spiced seasoning to what the rest of you are eating. (Omitting extra salt from everyone else's meal isn't such a bad idea for your family's health either.) When adding liquid to the food to make a smooth consistency, something nutritious is a better choice than plain water, although water will do. The water in which you steamed the vegetables is a good choice because it still contains some of the lost nutrients. You might also choose milk, juice, soup stock, or meat juice— depending, of course, on what it is you're preparing. Beware of items such as stock made from soup cubes which contain a heavy dose of sodium and very little nutrition.

> For recipes and suggestions on making your own babyfood, try *Feed Me! I'm Yours*, by Vicki Lansky (Bantam Books, New York: 1977). If you eliminate the salt from the toddler food recipes, chances are your child won't notice the difference (although you might).

If one meal at a time doesn't suit your style, you can prepare a larger quantity of food in advance and freeze it. Prepare the food as you would if you were going to serve it at the next meal. Then divide it into serving size quantities for future use. Servings can be quick-frozen in globs on a cookie sheet or piece of heavy duty aluminum foil, or in ice cube trays with individual popout containers. Place each frozen serving in a plastic wrap or little plastic bag, and store it in your freezer for up to a month. Thaw in the refrigerator. Room temperature thawing encourages bacteria growth.

When your child first begins solid foods you'll want to puree your babyfood concoctions to a very smooth consistency. By the time your child is eight months old or so, such preparation is no longer necessary or even completely desirable. Gradually introduce little lumps to your child's food to help ease the transition to the family table. It's important for your child to begin to use the gums and whatever teeth there are for chewing. If you confine your child's diet to absolutely smooth substances for too long, you may have trouble introducing lumps and rough textures later on.

BABY-SITTERS

There really aren't any firm rules for selecting a good baby-sitter. You have to do what makes sense for you. Here are some suggestions. (See also Day Care, page 52.)

• If you are lucky enough to have an extended family—grandparents, aunts or uncles, or other close relatives—they may be a good choice. This depends, of course, on the particular people involved. While many grandparents are delighted to help, others feel that they have raised their children and it's time for a rest. Don't take advantage of the good nature of family members. Remember that a mobile baby or toddler can be extremely taxing to a caregiver.

• Don't leave a mobile baby or toddler with a very young or inexperienced teenager. You know how quickly things can go wrong. It's best if the baby-sitter has the maturity and judgment to handle a crisis.

• Sources of baby-sitters include recommendations from friends, local church or community groups, your doctor, or other professionals.

• Interview before you hire. The person who worked perfectly for your best friend's child might be a disaster in your home.

• Make very clear just what you expect your baby-sitter to do. If you are not there, then the primary responsibility involves keeping your child comfortable and safe. Don't expect a childcare expert, housecleaner, laundress, and maintenance engineer all rolled into one.

• Make clear right from the start what your house rules are so that there won't be any misunderstandings. If you don't want your sitter to have visitors, use the telephone for personal calls, play your stereo, or consume the contents of your refrigerator, say so. (It's almost always a bad idea for a sitter to entertain in your home. Your child should receive the sitter's full attention.)

• Try having a person take care of your child when you are home for a short time. You can tell a lot this way. If things go well, you'll feel better about leaving your baby or toddler with that person when you need to go out. This will give you a chance to point out things in your home that the sitter should know about.

• Especially for a toddler who is able to manipulate a caregiver, establish the childcare procedures you feel are important. Share them with your child and the sitter together. For example, if bedtime in your house is at a fixed time, see that the sitter knows this and the child understands it's bedtime as usual. If on the other hand, your lifestyle is more flexible, tell the sitter that. There's no point in having a conflict between the child who is used to staying up until fatigue sets in and a sitter who thinks toddlers should be sound asleep at seven.

• If feeding your child is part of the arrangement, make sure the sitter knows what to use and how to prepare the meal. If snacks are permitted, have them available. If there are things you don't want your child to eat, tell the sitter. It's probably a good safety precaution to have a part-time sitter use as few appliances as possible. Heating up a prepared meal is probably as great as the sitter's involvement in the kitchen should be. (This might differ for full-time household help.) The food processor and other potentially dangerous items should not be in use with your toddler hanging about. A curious child may try to do things with a sitter that he or she wouldn't dare attempt with a parent. If there is any special information about your family's eating habits that the sitter should know, be sure to pass it on. (For example, if you keep a kosher home, or if you are vegetarians, don't assume that a new baby-sitter would know how to deal with this without instructions.)

• Be sure to provide whatever emergency information is necessary. Make sure the sitter knows what to do and whom to call if something goes wrong. Leave a number where you can be reached. If you can't do this, the sitter should know how to reach a reliable neighbor, relative, or friend.

• If you're not happy about a childcare arrangement you've made, change it. Remember, it's *your* child and *your* responsibility.

> *Dear Babysitter*, by Vicki Lansky (Meadowbrook Press, Deephaven, MN: 1982) is a useful handbook for sitters. It contains a refillable pad with spaces for telephone numbers and any special instructions you should leave with the sitter before going out. If you use a page each time you leave your child with a sitter, you'll be sure you haven't forgotten to provide the necessary information.

BABY-TALK

As time goes on, a baby's babbling sounds gradually become words, phrases, and sentences. At every stage of your child's language development, it's important for you to talk to and converse with your child. However, it's neither necessary nor especially desirable for you to mimic the way he or she speaks. Use conversational language that is natural and comfortable for *you* rather than baby-talk when you talk to your child. This will provide the best model and social stimulation to encourage your child's language development.

Although baby-talk shouldn't be your way of speaking, it's fine for your child. Try very hard to understand and respond to the words a baby or toddler invents in an attempt to tell you something. Don't correct the words or syntax to make the child say things "the right way." You say things the way *you* say them and let your child's language development progress at its own speed. Reward your child's early efforts to use language, even if that language may be a bit difficult to decipher. Go right ahead and give a bottle to a child who says, "Me bah pease." You know perfectly well what the child means. Trying to get the child to say "Give me my bottle, please," will be wasted energy as far as language development is concerned. What such pressure might accomplish, however, is helping to create a frustrated child who can't understand why you aren't delighted with his or her efforts to communicate.

BACKPACKS

There probably will be quite a few months between the time your baby outgrows a front pack carrier or infant carry basket and when he or she can walk rapidly and long enough to keep up with you as you move from place to place. Some parents find a backpack carrier to be very useful. Others skip it entirely and prefer to use a stroller. If you are considering a backpack, here are some points to keep in mind.

• Before you buy a backpack, try it on with your child in it. Will this way of transporting your baby or toddler be something you find convenient? Will a backpack suit your lifestyle?

• Make sure there's a safety strap to keep your child in the seat even against his or her will.

• Is the carrier comfortable for your back and is it roomy enough for your child?

• Are the shoulder straps strong, wide, and well padded?

• Is the frame strong but lightweight enough to be comfortable?

• Are you able to manage the pack on your own? Will you be able to load and unload your child without help?

If a backpack meets your family's needs, by all means buy one and enjoy using it. If it doesn't suit your personal style, don't feel that you need one to be a good parent. There are other ways to transport your child.

BATHS

A bath can and should be a pleasant experience for a child. A child's bath can be a pleasant experience for a parent as well. It's best to keep baths relatively simple. They needn't become major productions, sources of conflict, or the highlight of a day's entertainment. Try not to lose sight of the fact that the major purpose of a bath is to get your child clean, although this does not preclude having fun while bathing. A daily bath isn't essential as long as the diaper area and your child's hands and face are clean. How often your child needs a bath depends on how busy the child is and what the day's activities have been. Busier usually means more frequent baths.

Some Dos For the Bath

• If you're using the big tub, five or six inches of water at most is all you'll need. The bath water should feel comfortably warm (not hot) to your elbow or wrist. (Your hands can probably stand much hotter water than your child can, so hands are not a good test.)

• Even if your child has become too big for a real bath in the sink or dishpan, the bathroom or kitchen sink may still be a handy place for a quick dunk to clean the child's bottom.

• To keep your child from slipping in the large tub, try a towel or rubber mat on the tub's bottom. A large plastic laundry basket inside the tub works well to create a confined and relatively slip-proof space for an active child. Just put the basket in and fill the tub as usual. The water goes right through the holes. Then put your child into the basket.

• Kneel on something comfortable and get right down to your child's level. It's difficult and risky to hold or bathe your child while bending over. Until your child is very stable and able to sit securely, always support him or her with at least one hand, preferably two. One accidental slip in water can cause weeks of bathtime fears.

• Give your child a washcloth and let him or her help with the cleaning process. A small piece of soap tied into a child's sock makes an excellent cleaning tool for small hands to use.

• Use a mild soap. Ivory, a family favorite for many years, works well and it still floats. Special baby lotion soaps are fine if you don't mind the cost. Expensive perfumed adult toilet soaps are wasted on your child and may even cause skin irritation. Save them for yourself.

• Toys in the bath are fine, but don't overdo it. A few things that float and something to pour with are all your child needs. A delightful example of a commercially produced bathtub toy is "3 Men in a Tub," from Fisher Price. However, if you don't wish to spend money on bath toys, a plastic cup or two from the kitchen and an empty plastic shampoo bottle will keep a child busy.

• The bathroom should be warm enough so that your child doesn't get chilled in the bath. If the room is cool, make the bath a very quick one and get the child dry and warm right away when you're done.

• If the room is comfortable, time to play in the tub is fine, as long as you're willing to be right there and participate. It's best to stop the bath while it's still fun for both of you. Remember that there's going to be a next time very soon. For a child who wants to stay in the tub after you think the bath is ended, try a timer. Tell the child that when the bell rings the bath is over. Then stick to your word. Remove the child and let the water out.

Some Don'ts for the Bath

• Never run water into the tub or sink while the child is in it. An unexpected temperature change could cause harm. (Keep your child away from the hot water tap. If the tap remains hot while off, wrap it in a cool washcloth.)

• Never leave a baby or toddler unattended in the bath even for a minute. A young child can drown in as little as two inches of water, and it doesn't take very long for an accident to happen.

• Don't let your child get started on the bubble bath routine, especially using bath preparations intended for adults. The detergents in many of these products can cause skin irritation. For many active children it's difficult if not impossible to keep bits of the bath out of the mouth and eyes, and bubbles do no good in either of these places. Furthermore, if you start using the bubbles as a bribe to entice a child into the tub you're setting up a problem for the day you run out of bubbles. It's not worth it, although as a special and occasional treat a bubble bath can be fun.

• Don't let the water run out of the tub before you remove your child if yours is one of the many children frightened by the sight and sound of water going down the drain. Remember to empty the tub after the bath is over and you've removed the child. Don't leave a tub of water as a hazard for your mobile baby or toddler.

• Don't bathe siblings together unless you can count on good behavior. A toddler just learning to love the bath can be severely set back by one push from an older brother or sister. You know your children best. Do what makes sense, but keep in mind that group bathing may not save time in the long run.

Bathtime Fears

Fear of the bath may suddenly become a problem for a child who previously seemed to love getting into the tub. Sometimes a direct cause of the problem can be identified: soap in the eyes, an unfortunate slip under the water, a newly discovered awareness of the water going down the drain. In some children, however, the fear will have no obvious cause, but one day will simply appear.

If your child is one of those who develops a fear of the bath, keep in mind that force will not solve the problem but will probably make it worse. Putting a terrified child into the tub will not get him or her used to the water. Keep the child clean with sponge baths while you work on the fears gradually. Here are some suggestions for getting a frightened child to trust the water again.

• Go back to using a small container and don't try to bathe a tiny tot in a large tub. Put the child on a plastic tablecloth on the floor next to a small basin or dishpan with an inch or two of water. Let the child play with a floating toy and put the hands into the water if he or she wishes. Using a cloth or a small sponge, wash the child gently. Be careful not to get soap in the eyes. If the child wants to climb into the pan, let it happen. Provide support so there's no slipping or falling.

• After you've achieved success with water play on the floor, try moving the basin into the large tub. Let the child sit in the empty tub next to the pan of water and play as before. Letting the pan of water spill out into the big tub can be fun and the start again of real baths. Make this move only when you're sure the child is ready.

• If fear of going down the drain is a problem, be careful not to begin to empty the tub while your child is in the room. Silly as that fear may seem to you, many children do genuinely believe that they will go down with the water and no amount of reasoning will get a toddler who thinks so to believe otherwise.

• If you have a hand held shower, you might try letting your child sit in an empty tub and spray off the soap you have applied with a wet cloth. Be careful to regulate water temperature and pressure carefully, and don't try this approach if your plumbing tends toward bursts of hot water. Some children will be delighted with the notion of a shower. Others will hate it. Don't force.

BEDS AND BEDDING

Cribs

Most children sleep in a crib for at least the first two years and many continue to use a crib for another year or two after that. All new full-sized cribs now sold in the United States must meet safety requirements established by the Consumer Product Safety Commission. Here are some points to keep in mind if you borrow or purchase a secondhand crib that could have been manufactured before the regulations were adopted.

• The bars in the sides of the crib should be no farther apart than 2⅜". Even if you're sure your child's head can't fit through the spaces, it's important that a slender body not be able to squeeze through sideways. Children have been known to hang themselves by trying to exit feet-first through the bars.

• The mattress should fit tightly with no room for a child to squeeze between it and the sides.

• Surfaces should be nontoxic and splinter-free.

• Hardware should be safe and secure. There shouldn't be any sharp parts, things that could break off, or movable features that move when they're not supposed to.

• Decorative features, if any, must be safe. There should be nothing that could trap or injure a child. Beware of carved-out panels which might permit a child to get caught between a post and part of the panel.

Bedding

Fitted sheets are convenient because they stay put. Patterned sheets are pretty and give your child something interesting to look at. Avoid using any pillows in the crib. Children don't need pillows for comfortable sleeping, and soft pillows could present a smothering hazard.

Crib bumpers which soften the crib sides and keep out drafts are fine for young babies. However, some children, once they can stand, use the bumper as a step to climb out. It's safer to remove the bumper as soon as your child has figured out this new use for it.

After the Crib

When and how should you move a child from a crib to a regular bed? Here are some suggestions.

• If your child has taken to climbing and falling out of the crib, sooner rather than later is the time to give up the crib altogether. At least leave the crib side down and the mattress in the lowest position so your climber won't have as far to fall. Pillows on the landing side might be wise.

• Unless your house is especially drafty, the mattress on the floor is a good transition from crib to regular bed for a child who climbs and falls out.

• Remember that once your child can get out of crib or bed freely, his or her night wandering could occur without your knowledge. Make sure that your child only has access to childproofed places if he or she should stray without waking you.

• Easy-to-install temporary sides can be purchased for regular beds to help keep a young child from rolling out while sleeping. (These will not keep an awake child in bed, however.) One side of the bed against the wall and two chairs on the other side will do in a pinch.

• If you are expecting another baby, don't force your older child to give up the crib for the new arrival. Expecting your toddler to accept a newborn sibling graciously is demanding enough without requiring the older child to give up his or her sleeping place at the same time. Either make the transition out of the crib far enough in advance so there's no relation between giving up the crib and the new baby's arrival, or buy a second crib.

BEDTIME (Early or Late?)

A newborn sleeps most of the time, wakens when hungry or uncomfortable, and then returns to sleep after being fed. Once your baby begins to sleep through the night and to be awake at times other than feedings, you'll have to work out a plan for naps and bedtime.

When should a child go to bed? There is no one right answer to that question. Decide the best time for your family based on your child's needs and your lifestyle. For some, "early to bed and early to rise" is the most satisfactory approach. It suits other families to enjoy the company of their toddler well into the evening so that everyone can sleep later the next morning. For some families a very regular schedule works best. For others variety seems to do no harm. Use common sense and figure out what's best for you and your child. Don't be intimidated by the opinions of those whose lifestyle differs from your own. There is no one bedtime that is right for every child. Chances are, for the first two years at least, you can count on your child to take as much sleep as necessary. Most very young children do. You'll be able to tell if your child is overtired. If so, encourage extra or longer naps.

Some people really do seem to be larks (early risers) while others tend to be owls (nightbirds). If you're lucky, your child's personal style will be similar to your own. If not, you may want to make efforts to modify your child's sleeping and waking schedule, although such efforts may not be entirely successful. For a child who wakes too early, gradually make bedtime later. Move bedtime back fifteen minutes each night until you are keeping the child up late enough to sleep through till a more reasonable hour of morning. If you want your child to go to bed earlier, make sure that the day has been active enough so that need for sleep (but not overtiredness) works for you. Gradually begin the bedtime rituals earlier each night until you've established a time you find suitable. Do what makes sense to you. The key to success is not to make a big deal out of it.

BEDTIME RITUALS

Whatever type of schedule—fixed or flexible—you use for your child's bedtime, the routines you employ to establish that it is in fact that time of night should be a predictable aspect of the child's life. The rituals which accompany bedtime can help your child feel secure despite the fact that bedtime involves separation. Making bedtime a comfortable experience on which a child can rely will help prevent sleep problems and enable the child to take important steps toward independence.

Begin bedtime rituals at least a half hour before you want to have the child settled for the night. Don't rush and convey the impression that you can't wait to get it all over with. Include whatever practices suit your child's needs and your family's lifestyle. Many children will enjoy saying goodnight to the people, goodnight to the animals, and goodnight to the familiar objects. Include, if you wish, tucking in the dolls or stuffed toys. Getting the child out of the clothes of the day and into pajamas for sleeping may include a bath in the process if necessary. A bedtime story or perhaps two, and prayers if you are religious, can complete the ritual. What's important is that the routine you establish should vary little from night to night. The bedtime ritual should inevitably signal bedtime and give your child a secure sense that some things in life can be counted on without disappointment.

When you have finished with whatever routine you have established for bedtime, tuck your child in, give him or her a goodnight kiss, and leave the room. Don't get into the habit of staying around until your child has fallen asleep, because once you build that practice into the bedtime ritual, you'll find it difficult to change. For a child who protests being left alone, frequent but very brief appearances at his or her bedside for reassurance are in order. This is a reasonable middle ground between letting a child "cry it out" and letting a child manipulate you into becoming a sleepy-time companion. It also seems to be the most effective way to encourage peaceful separation at bedtime. (See Family Beds, page 66; and Sleep Problems, page 118.)

BED-WETTING

Bed-wetting should not be considered a problem behavior for a toddler. It's completely normal. Many children—even those who are perfectly toilet trained during the day—do not remain dry at night until they are three or even four years old. For some children dry nights take even longer than that.

Don't be concerned about using diapers at night, even for a child who successfully wears training pants all day. If you avoid making an issue of bed-wetting, your child is likely to outgrow it sooner. Creating tension at bedtime is a sure way to make bed-wetting persist. Remember that your child does not *deliberately* wet the bed. He or she is asleep when it happens. So punishment is not appropriate for wetting. Praise is not needed or appropriate for staying dry. The less you make of the matter the sooner normal development will take over and your child will stay dry.

If your child continues to wet the bed long after you think he or she should have stopped, consult your pediatrician. Chances are you will be reassured that time will take care of it. If there is some reason for concern in your particular situation, the doctor can make suggestions to deal with the problem. (See also Toilet Training and Toilet Learning, page 134.)

BIBS

For a baby who's not yet taking solid foods, a terrycloth bib with plastic backing works well to keep spilled milk or juice off the child's clothes. Best are the bibs that snap in back rather than tie. If you use a bib that ties, be sure to remove it immediately after feeding. Never leave an infant with anything tied around the neck.

For a baby or toddler who's self-feeding (more or less), a bib of heavy plastic with a deep pocket at the bottom is the best choice. It protects the clothes and catches the spills—liquid and solid—in the pocket. Be sure to wash out the pocket carefully after each use. Failure to do so is likely to result in a mess that smells and looks bad. And, if you don't keep the bib clean, your toddler is likely to be adding spoiled remnants of last night's dinner to today's lunch.

BITES (Treatment)

Animal or Human Bites

Wash the area well with soap and room-temperature water. If the bitten spot is not bleeding badly, let the water run gently over it for a few minutes. Control severe bleeding by putting direct pressure on the wound. When the bleeding has stopped, cleanse the area with Mercurochrome or a similar antiseptic and cover the wound with a sterile dressing. Call a physician for advice the same day. Make sure your child's tetanus immunization is up to date.

If the bite is from an animal, it's best to capture the animal if you can so that it can be checked to make sure it's not rabid. If someone else's pet has bitten your child, you should notify the owner. Your local animal shelter will help if you can't locate the owner. It's important that the health of the animal that bit your child be checked.

Call your child's doctor for advice about a human bite. The bacteria in a person's mouth can cause the bite wound to become infected.

For the next week or so, watch the site of the bite very carefully to make sure it doesn't become infected. If you see swelling and redness, or your child develops a fever, call the doctor and report this.

Insect Bites and Stings

If there's a stinger, it's probably best to leave it alone and let the doctor remove it. Touching it may release more venom and increase the reaction. If you must remove the stinger on your own, scrape it out with a fingernail. You may get a wee bit of skin, but that's preferable to leaving the stinger in there. A little meat tenderizer and water on the bite may help draw out the venom. Check this out with the doctor. Apply cold compresses, and watch the child carefully for any reaction to the bite. Call the doctor right away if the child becomes pale or weak, or develops a rash or hives, fever, trouble breathing, nausea, or vomiting.

Snake Bites

If you live in an area where there are poisonous snakes, be especially alert to the possibility that your child might be bitten. If you think your child has been bitten by a poisonous snake (you will usually be able to see one or more fang marks in the skin) call the doctor immediately or take your child to the nearest emergency room. The bite of a poisonous snake requires medical treatment. If poisonous snakes are common in your area, ask your doctor to tell you what home treatment you should follow before you get to the hospital if your child is bitten. If your child stops breathing, begin artificial respiration. (See Breathing Emergency, page 34.)

BITING

Biting other people is not acceptable behavior, and if your child shows signs of becoming a biter it's best to deal with this promptly and firmly.

If it's other children who are being bitten, try to avoid the situations where this occurs. Don't permit children to play together without close supervision. If the biting accompanies fighting over toys or other objects, make sure that there are enough playthings to go around. At the first move toward a bite, remove your child bodily from the temptation. Say "No. Don't bite."

If it's you your child bites, a sharp "No" while firmly restraining the child will communicate that you are displeased. A baby who bites the mother's breast while nursing should be told "No" and removed momentarily from the breast.

Resist the impulse to strike the child who bites or to bite back. Such retaliation is more likely to set a bad example than to act as a deterrent. The child may figure out that biting hurts, but he or she will also get the message that it's all right to bite or hit someone.

If biting or other symptoms of aggressive behavior seem to be a continuing problem with your child, consult your pediatrician. You may need help dealing with the underlying causes. (See also Aggressive Behavior, page 10.)

BLEEDING

Use direct pressure with a clean cloth (for up to 15 minutes) to stop bleeding from cuts or bites. An ice cube wrapped in the cloth may be useful. Get immediate medical attention if the bleeding doesn't stop within 15 minutes. For a very deep wound from which the blood is spurting rapidly (severed artery) apply direct pressure using your fist if necessary to press the severed blood vessel hard against an underlying bone. Meanwhile, have someone call for help.

BOOKS

Books are an important part of a child's learning experiences, as well as one of life's pleasures, and it's never too soon to begin sharing them with your child. Begin today, if you haven't already. Even a newborn will enjoy the sounds of a parent's voice reading, and many children can begin to understand words and follow a story long before you might think that's possible.

Books for Fun

Begin by reading *your* favorites to your child so that your enthusiasm shows. To help you get started choosing books for your toddler, here are some of Ánna Máire's (and her mother's) favorites. A few of the titles are repeated from *Welcome Baby*'s list of suggestions.

The Poky Little Puppy, by Janette Sebring Lowrey
Western Publishing Co., Racine Wisconsin: 1942, 1970
A fun story with a lesson too. If you let your child help you count the puppies, it won't be long before he or she can count to five.

Bread and Jam for Frances, by Russell Hoban
Harper & Row Publishers, New York: 1964
If your toddler is a fussy eater, this story will be good for both of you. An enjoyable book even for eager eaters.

The Roly-Poly Pudding, by Beatrix Potter
Frederick Warne & Co., Inc. New York: 1908
Along with *The Tale of Peter Rabbit*, this is one of Ánna Máire's favorite books by Beatrix Potter. The complete set of 23 titles (many available in paperback) is well worth having. There are modern editions, but we still prefer the little books with Beatrix Potter's own pictures, as originally published by Frederick Warne.

Winnie-The-Pooh, by A. A. Milne, illustrated by E.H. Shepard
E.P. Dutton & Co., Inc. New York: 1926
This children's classic provides many bedtime stories, and you can stop at virtually any point and promise more for tomorrow. We like the original version with E.H. Shepard's decorations.

The Little Fur Family, by Margaret Wise Brown
Harper & Row Publishers, New York: 1946
The book jacket says, "A warm little story, simple enough for the very very young child to take to his heart." We agree.

Corduroy, by Don Freeman
The Viking Press, New York: 1968
Corduroy is a bear in a toy department who finds a friend and a home. A nice, reassuring story for young children.

The Lorax, by Dr. Seuss
Random House, Inc., New York: 1971
This is our favorite Dr. Seuss title. Marvelous rhythm and rhyme for reading aloud, and a message to set us all thinking.

Alexander and the Terrible, Horrible, No Good, Very Bad Day, by Judith Viorst
Atheneum, New York: 1972
There are days like this in our house. Probably even in your house too. An amusing story to make any day not quite so bad.

Where the Wild Things Are, by Maurice Sendak
Harper & Row Publishers, New York: 1963
A wonderful story to read aloud to a contrary toddler. The Caldecott award-winning illustrations will hold a child's attention.

Goodnight Moon, by Margaret Wise Brown
Harper & Row Publishers, New York: 1947
One of Ánna Máire's favorite bedtime stories. Saying "goodnight" can become an important part of any child's bedtime ritual.

A Tree is Nice, by Janice May Udry, pictures by Marc Simont
Harper & Row Publishers, New York: 1956
This Caldecott winner has all the reasons that trees are nice, in simple words and lovely pictures. Be prepared to help your child plant a tree when you're done with the book.

Three Bedtime Stories, pictures by Garth Williams
Golden Press, Racine, Wisconsin: 1958
Three popular bedtime stories, each starring three animal characters: the three little kittens, the three little pigs, and the three bears. These familiar tales are nicely presented with lovely illustrations.

Katy No-Pocket, by Emmy Payne, pictures by H.A. Rey
Houghton Mifflin Company, Boston: 1944
An entertaining story about how Katy Kangaroo obtains a pocket to carry her child. This children's classic has stood the test of time.

Flip, story and pictures by Wesley Dennis
The Viking Press, New York: 1941
A wonderful story of dreaming, growing, trying, and succeeding. If Flip were a person, he'd be a toddler. He's a horse, but the message is for children.

The Snowy Day, by Ezra Jack Keats
The Viking Press, New York: 1962
Another Caldecott winner, with artwork to delight you and your child. Your toddler will learn what happens when you try to save a snowball in your pocket until tomorrow.

Waiting, by Nicki Weiss
Greenwillow Books, New York: 1981
A simple, sensitively written story that reassuringly deals with separation anxiety and Mama's return.

Gilberto and the Wind, by Marie Hall Ets
The Viking Press, New York: 1963
A beautiful and instructive tale. Children, like Gilberto, will enjoy listening to the wind and watching its effects.

Reading Readiness

Interest in books is an important ingredient of reading readiness, and sharing books with your child will pay off later when he or she goes to school. As you read, let your child look at the page with you. Encourage your child to talk about the pictures and, if you wish, point out a word or two. Remember, however, that pleasure is the major purpose of reading with your child at this point, and it's too soon to teach reading in a formal way. Just enjoy.

BOTTLES

If you are bottle feeding your child, chances are you'll have all your routines worked out by the time you read this book. For a guide to bottle-feeding a newborn baby, see pages 29-34 of *Welcome Baby: A Guide to the First Six Weeks,* by Anne Marie Mueser and George E. Verrilli, (St. Martin's Press, New York: 1982).

In *Talk & Toddle,* see also Nutrition, page 98; Feeding (How and When), page 69; Weaning (From the Breast), page 149; Weaning (From the Bottle), page 147.

BOWEL MOVEMENTS

By the time you read this, you've probably changed enough diapers to know what a normal bowel movement for your child is. The frequency of bowel movements varies greatly from one child to another. Some babies, particularly breast-fed ones, have several movements a day. Others might only have a movement every two or three days. A daily movement is not necessary. Most young children move their bowels when they need to. If your child is eating well, acting normally, and passing a stool without difficulty, then it doesn't matter whether he or she is having several bowel movements a day or one bowel movement every several days.

Constipation

Constipation is seldom a problem in a young baby, especially one who is breast-fed. Make sure that an older baby or toddler has enough juice or fruit in the diet. Never tamper with a child's normal pattern of bowel movements by administering a laxative (unless your doctor specifically prescribes one at a particular time). As a rule, children don't need laxatives, and upsetting a child's natural rhythm will do no good; it may cause harm by starting a dependence on the laxative. Infrequent bowel movements are not a sign of constipation or cause for concern as long as the stools are reasonably soft when they are passed.

If your child does pass small, rabbit-pellet type of stools, this indicates constipation. In most cases, this situation can be corrected by giving dark Karo syrup (1 teaspoon to 4 ounces of water) once or twice a day. Check with your doctor first. You may also cut down on the milk and increase the juice for a day or two. If your child appears very uncomfortable or appears to be straining too much with a bowel movement, stimulation with a rectal thermometer may help.

Diarrhea

How can you tell if your child has diarrhea or simply the frequent, loose bowel movements common to many children? A child with diarrhea passes stools that have little or no formed material in them. They usually differ in color from normal stools. The stools are more frequent than usual, noisy, and passed with considerable force. They may contain mucus or blood.

The most serious danger from diarrhea is dehydration which in severe cases can be fatal for a very young child. Call your pediatrician immediately if your child seems to have diarrhea with one or more of these other symptoms: mucus or blood in the stools, vomiting, temperature below 97.6 or above 99.6 degrees F., lack of appetite, decreased quantity of urine, dry mouth (no saliva), no tears when crying, decreased energy and activity level.

BREAST-FEEDING (Duration)

How long should a nursing mother continue to breast-feed her baby? This is a decision that is best made by mother and child together. It really isn't anyone else's business, although many people seem willing to offer unsolicited advice on this topic. And, no matter when you wean your child, there will be people who think it's too soon and others who wonder why you waited so long. There isn't one right answer to the question "How long should a mother breast-feed her baby?" You should do whatever makes sense to you in your particular circumstances. Here are some things to consider as you make your decision.

• If you stop breast-feeding after two months or so (if, for example, you return to a full time job or simply choose to stop nursing), don't feel guilty about it. You've already given your baby a good start and he or she is likely to continue to thrive if you switch to bottles. The baby should be held during feedings and you must make an extra effort to maintain some of that special closeness you and your baby developed as a nursing couple.

• Between six and nine months, many babies spontaneously show that they are ready to begin giving up the breast. They may appear disinterested or nurse only briefly. They may, all of a sudden, reject the breast completely. If your baby persistently sends you these signals, you'll probably realize that weaning time has arrived whether or not you would have planned it that way.

• If you are still nursing by the end of the first year, chances are that much of the child's nourishment is coming from other sources. Some mothers and babies choose to continue the nursing relationship into the second year (or even longer) even after solid foods have been introduced and nursing is no longer essential for meeting the child's nutritional needs. If you wish to continue to breast-feed your child beyond the time needed for physical nourishment, that is your decision. Just be aware that the primary needs being met no longer involve food for your child's body. Emotional security and satisfaction, and comfort needs — both yours and your child's — have taken over. Be sure that your desire to continue the nursing relationship meets your child's needs as well as your own. (See Weaning, page 149.)

BREATH HOLDING

Some children use holding the breath as a device during a temper tantrum. The sight of a toddler stopping breathing long enough to turn blue and even lose consciousness momentarily is a very alarming one. However, these episodes generally leave no ill effects on the child, although they may create considerable anxiety in the parents.

If breath-holding spells are part of your child's temper tantrum stratagems, be careful not to overreact. Be reassured that a child won't (can't) stop breathing long enough to cause serious physical harm. However, if you permit yourself to be manipulated and controlled by such tantrum behavior, your child's developing personality as well as your relationship may be affected. If a child finds that breath holding works to get what he or she wants, you are likely to find it occurring more often. Deal with the temper tantrum as you would have if it had taken any other form. (See Tantrums, page 125.)

Consult your child's pediatrician if the breath-holding spell seems to be part of a convulsion or if it is very severe or prolonged.

BREATHING EMERGENCY

When a person stops breathing for any reason—drowning, blocked air passage, electric shock, poisonous bite, or any other reason—this should be considered a life-threatening emergency which requires immediate help.

Never give artificial respiration (rescue breathing) to a person who is breathing. Here are steps to follow if your child has stopped breathing for more than ten seconds. Don't waste any time getting on with it. Continue until the child is breathing well on his or her own or until expert help arrives.

If drowning causes the problem, begin with Step 1. If not, begin with Step 2.

(1) First get the water out of the child's lungs. To do this, hold the baby face down with the head lower than the rest of the body.

(2) Use a hooked finger to clear the child's mouth of mucus, food, or anything else that shouldn't be there.

(3) Place the child on his or her back, on a flat surface.

(4) Tilt the child's head back (neck stretched, chin up, jaw forward) to keep the air passages open.

(5) With your mouth, cover the baby's mouth and nose tightly. Breathe a small puff of air gently into the baby's nose and mouth just enough to make the chest wall move up a little. (Remember that a baby is very small, and couldn't handle the entire contents of your lungs at once.)

(6) Move away so the air can come out. Put your mouth back and breathe another puff of air; then move away. Do this every three seconds (20 times a minute) until the baby begins to breathe well or help comes.

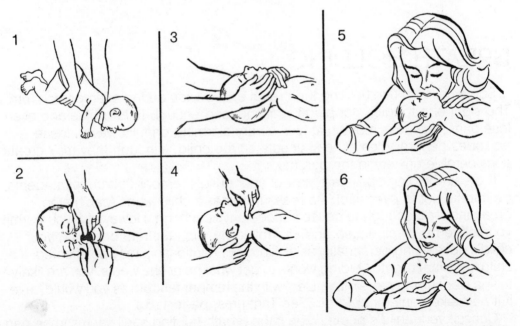

Reprinted with permission from *Welcome Baby: A Guide to the First Six Weeks,* by Anne Marie Mueser and George E. Verrilli, (St. Martin's Press, New York: 1982).

34

These steps (in which you cover both the mouth and nose with your mouth) are designed for a baby, toddler, or child up to about the age of eight. For older children or adults place your mouth only over the victim's mouth and pinch the nostrils together between your index finger and thumb.

Rescue breathing procedures are best learned from experts. Take a first aid course or at least a course in Cardiopulmonary Resuscitation (CPR) if you can.

BURNS AND SCALDS

To prevent burns or scalds, make sure that your mobile baby doesn't have access to hot things. Don't place objects like coffeepots on surfaces where a toddler could pull them down. Turn the pot handles away from the edge of the stove when you are cooking. Never leave an unattended mobile baby or toddler in a room where there is an open fire or space heater, a stove in use, or a hot iron. Keep matches out of sight and out of reach. If your tap water is hot enough to scald (above 125° F.), adjust it. If you can't adjust it, make sure that your child does not have access to the taps at any time.

If your child does suffer a burn or scald, here's what to do: Cool the injured area as fast as possible by dunking the burned part in cold water or applying cold compresses. Continue to apply cold for several minutes until the pain stops. Then pat the skin dry very gently with the cleanest cloth or towel you can find. Keep the burned area loosely covered. Don't use adhesive. Don't break blisters, and don't apply creams, ointments, greases, butter, jellies, or antiseptics. Call your child's doctor for advice on what to do next.

In the case of a chemical burn, wash the area thoroughly with water—lots of water. The sooner you get the chemical off the child's skin the sooner the damage will stop and healing can begin. Hold the child under a cold water faucet or hose if necessary. Then remove the clothes and continue to wash with cold water. After you've got all the chemical washed off, call the doctor right away. (See also Accidents (Prevention), page 7.)

CANDY AND SWEETS

Sweets are not good for a person's teeth. Many parents try to minimize any contact their children have with candy or similar treats. While avoiding sweets altogether is certainly best for your child's teeth, you may not be willing or able to enforce that. Most people do find sweets to be pleasurable. Even newborn babies, if offered both sweetened water and plain, tend to suck longer on the bottles with sugar. How should you handle the issue of sweets with your child? Here are some suggestions.

• If you do permit sweets, remember that those which remain in the mouth the least amount of time will cause the least harm. For example, a piece of a chocolate bar which melts quickly is better than a long-lasting lollipop. Chewy gumdrops which leave particles in the teeth are more harmful than candies which dissolve rapidly.

• Never give your baby a pacifier dipped in sugar, honey, or jelly.

• Chewing gum made with sugar should be avoided. (See page 38.)

• A handful of candy eaten quickly is better than that same handful consumed a bit at a time over several hours.

• A drink of water should follow sweets. The child's teeth should be brushed as soon as possible.

• Don't be fooled into thinking that dried fruits are a perfect substitute for candy. The unrefined sugar in these chewy fruits can cause harm if the particles remain in the mouth for any period of time.

• Remember it's not just candy that can cause problems. Desserts such as cake, ice cream, sweet puddings, or tarts should be followed by a drink of water and a tooth brushing.

• Don't serve presweetened cereal, which adds lots of decay-causing sugar and very little nutrition to the diet.

For many parents, the best approach to candy and other sweets is not to make a big deal about them. Don't encourage them, but don't make them so special that they become more enticing than they ordinarily would be. Forbidden sweets may be the sweetest of all. Sweets are nice to eat, and it's best to leave it at that. Avoid using them as props in your child-management strategies. Don't increase their appeal by making sweets into rewards for good behavior, soothers for minor childhood crises, or bribes to get your child to behave better. (See also Sugar, page 122.)

CAROTENEMIA

Does your child's skin—especially the palms of the hands and the soles of the feet—appear somewhat yellowish in color? This staining of the skin, a condition called carotenemia, is caused by the pigment carotene which is found in vegetables such as carrots, squash, and sweet potatoes. Carotenemia is harmless and quite common among children under the age of two, especially those who eat large quantities of commercially prepared baby and junior foods with a high percentage of carotene-containing ingredients.

Don't confuse carotenemia with jaundice, a condition which is considerably more serious. Carotenemia is only noticed in the thick layers of skin. Unlike jaundice, it is never seen in the whites of the eyes. If your child's eyes seem to be yellowish, consult a physician.

CEREALS

First Solid Food

The first solid food given to babies is most often a precooked dry infant cereal made from a single grain such as rice or barley. This type of cereal is prepared by mixing warm formula or water with the dry flakes. It provides essential nutrients, especially iron, which is lacking in the diet of a baby whose main source of food is mother's milk, or formula which isn't iron-fortified, or cow's milk. There is no particular advantage to cooking your own cereal for a baby. The cooking takes time, and adult cereals may not provide enough iron. Beware of precooked "instant" adult cereals to which you add boiling water. These usually contain added salt. The best cereal for a baby is a packaged infant cereal (iron fortified) to which you add formula or water.

Read the list of ingredients and the nutritional information before you buy. It's safer to stick to the plain infant cereals such as rice, barley, or oatmeal. The mixtures that already have fruit and dried formula cost more and may contain ingredients to which some children are sensitive. If your baby does react badly to a cereal mixture, you won't know which ingredient is causing the problem.

Don't add sugar or other sweetener to your baby's cereal even if *you* think it tastes awful. Serve it with a bit of pureed fruit (commercially prepared or homemade). Applesauce is a good one to start with. It's relatively easy to digest, and many babies seem to like it.

Cereals for Toddlers

Chosen wisely and served with milk, cereals can provide excellent nutrition for your toddler. Chosen by a child from the television commercials or supermarket displays, cereals could be the start of a toddler's junk food habit rather than a source of healthful meals. Before you buy a cereal for your toddler (or for yourself) read the ingredients list and nutritional information. Remember that ingredients are listed in the order of their importance in the particular product. A cereal which lists sugar first has more sugar than any other ingredient.

Avoid the "instant" hot cereals which have salt already added. Your toddler doesn't need the sodium, and it's a simple matter to cook the regular cereal without salt.

Labels like "all natural," "fortified," "high fiber," are obviously intended to convince you that the contents of a container are more nutritious than similar products which are not so labeled. Don't be easily fooled. For example, many of the granola cereal preparations, which convey the impression of high nutritional standards, are relatively high in calories for the nutrition provided, and they are sweeter than your child needs as well.

If you're going to serve a dry cereal, a whole grain cereal such as Kellogg's

Nutri-Grain is a good choice. Many toddlers like Cheerios, a cereal which provides excellent nutrition, although its sodium content is a bit higher than that of some other varieties. If your child likes Cheerios and you're careful about salt the rest of the time, don't worry about it. Always serve a dry cereal with milk, which provides calcium and additional protein.

Avoid the presweetened cereals and any which contain artificial colorings and flavorings. Among the worst offenders for sugar content are Apple Jacks, Cap'n Crunch, Lucky Charms, Cocoa Krispies, Cocoa Pebbles, Cookie-Crisp, Count Chocula, Froot Loops, Fruity Pebbles, Strawberry Shortcake, Sugar Frosted Flakes, Sugar Smacks, and Super Sugar Crisp. Each of these contains 40% or more sugar by weight. No matter how appealing the advertising and packaging may be, don't let your child manipulate you into purchasing these items. Fad cereals come and go, and some of the names on this list may well have been replaced by new ones by your next trip to the supermarket. Before you buy any cereal, check the nutritional label for sucrose carbohydrates (sugar content). If you feel that your child *must* have a sweetened cereal, purchase one of the nutritionally sound varieties and add a wee bit (less than a teaspoon) of sugar.

CHEWING (Learning How)

A baby's first chewing experience is with the gums, even before the chewing teeth come in. As soon as your baby can put the hands (and whatever they contain) to the mouth, he or she is beginning to learn the motions of chewing.

The first teeth a baby gets are front ones for biting. (See Teething, page 127.) These are not chewing teeth, but the baby is already gumming things in a chewing motion. As soon as your child begins a regular practice of putting things into the mouth, you should provide some hard food objects on which to practice chewing. Teething biscuits or Zwiebacks are excellent. It's best to give the baby the chewing experience on a hard real food such as a biscuit when the impulse to explore with the mouth is strong. If you don't, and serve nothing but pureed foods until the chewing teeth (molars) are well established, your child might resist having to chew to eat. Be careful, however, not to offer bits of apple or raw carrot until you are sure that your child can and will make the proper chewing motions. A baby with front teeth only could bite off and inhale a bit of apple. Don't let your baby chew on any food while lying down.

CHEWING GUM

You'll probably find it best for everyone concerned if your toddler does not chew gum. Gums flavored with sugar are very harmful to the teeth and definitely should be avoided. A wad of sugarless gum won't cause tooth decay, but it will (like any other kind) tend to seek out the most undesirable locations — a chair seat, the place you're about to put your foot, the dog's ear, or your child's hair.

No matter how careful you are, however, you probably won't have the good fortune in today's world to keep your child and chewing gum apart forever.

Even if your child doesn't chew, chances are a playmate will. Here are some hints to remove chewing gum from hair.

• Try cold cream, baby lotion, or baby oil. Massage it well into the area containing the wad of gum. Wait at least five minutes.

• After the cream has had a chance to penetrate, try to separate the hairs (which by now should be nice and slippery) a few at a time, from the gum.

• Shampoo to remove the remaining mess.

• If this doesn't work, probably nothing will. Resort to scissors.

CHILD ABUSE

Child abuse is not nice, but it happens. Many parents who abuse their children were themselves abused as youngsters, and they are parenting as did the examples they know well. When child abuse starts, it's often hard to stop it without help. Many abusive parents really do love their children and simply lose control. Some are not even aware of how damaging their actions are. Not all abusers are parents. Friends, relatives, baby-sitters and other caregivers have been known to hurt other people's children.

Many cases of child abuse involve physical harm—beating, battering, bruising, burning, or otherwise causing pain or physical injury. Physical neglect —failing to nourish, clothe, clean, or otherwise care for a child—is also a form of abuse. Some children are abused sexually. Verbal abuse—screaming, ridicule, constant fault finding—can cause emotional damage and may escalate into physical abuse.

Abuse of a young baby often starts as a desperate reaction to constant crying and the frustration of being unable to quiet the child. Abuse of a toddler or older child is likely to be discipline and punishment that's gotten out of hand. Toddlers are especially vulnerable to abuse because what is normal behavior for a toddler—curiosity, never-ending questions, exploration, abundant energy, contrariness, and dawdling—has the potential to provoke even the most easygoing adult to lose his or her temper. Anyone who says living with a toddler is easy probably hasn't tried it recently.

What should you do if your child seems to bring out the worst in you? Remember that no parent is perfect and that no matter how hard you try, there will be days when things will go wrong. Here are some warning signs to watch for if you seem to be having more bad days than good ones.

• Are your days full of conflict and combat with your child? Do you feel out of control? Do you feel that you can't cope a lot of the time?

• Do you scream at your child a lot? Do you find yourself thinking that he or she can't do anything right? Do you use ridicule and verbal putdowns?

• Do you frequently lose your temper with your child? Do you dish out discipline and punishment while in a fit of rage?

• When you lose your temper, do you hit, push, shake or otherwise touch your child in a way that might hurt him or her?

• Do you find yourself using punishment far more than praise for your child? Do you use or are you tempted to use punishment devices such as beating, tying the child up, locking the child in a room or closet?

• Do you find yourself resenting your child? Do you often wish that you didn't have any children?

If a "Yes" answer to any or all of the above questions would be the rule rather than the exception for you, do yourself and your child a favor and get some additional support to make life easier. Find someone you can trust—a friend, relative, or volunteer recommended by your church or community agency— and when things become unbearable, let that person stay with your child for an hour or two or more while you get out of the house. It's better to leave for a while than to stay and do something you'll regret.

> If you are abusing your child or if you're afraid you might, call the **Parents Anonymous** toll-free number
> Outside California 800-421-0353
> In California 800-352-0386
> Whenever you call, someone will answer, listen, and direct you to the help you need.

For a continuing source of support and communication find your local chapter of Parents Anonymous and go to a meeting. Look in the phone book, ask your child's doctor, or call the P.A. toll-free number for information. Parents Anonymous, which was founded by parents to help other parents stop hurting their children, has more than 800 chapters nationwide. Don't be embarrassed or afraid to call. You'll receive understanding and supportive help from people who know what you are going through. If you haven't abused your child yet, but feel that your ability to cope is gradually slipping away, you can call P.A. for suggestions *before* you lose control and hurt your child. Prevention now is better than repairing the damage later. Parents Anonymous is not a reporting agency, and no one will judge you or report you to authorities because you call and ask for help. You can call the toll-free number any hour of day or night, seven days a week. Do it if you need to.

CHILDPROOFING

If it appears to you that this book contains numerous and perhaps even repetitious references to techniques of keeping your baby or toddler safe, you're right. The world is full of interesting things that could cause harm to a child whose need to explore is not yet matched by good judgment. Childproofing your surroundings—especially for an energetic toddler—is a neverending process, or at least it seems that way. No matter how carefully you have gone over everything, your child may be creating a new way to get into trouble. That's an almost inevitable characteristic of toddlerhood.

To childproof your home effectively you must look at everything from the vantage point of someone your child's size. Just before your baby becomes mobile, you must concentrate on making safe everything within a crawler's reach. Chances are it's been a long time since you've had to focus so intently on the environment between your knees and the floor. As your child becomes bigger, stronger, and able to stand and climb, you must extend your childproofing efforts to everything he or she can reach or climb to reach.

There are devices you can purchase to help you make your home a safer place for your child. You may find it helpful to use safety latches for cupboards and drawers, cover plugs for unused electric outlets, foam tape for padding sharp edges, "childproof" lids for medications and household products, and safety gates to close off high risk areas such as stairways or forbidden rooms. Windows above the ground floor should have window guards.

Don't, however, depend on safety gimmicks to do the entire job no matter how effective they may seem to be. Be as careful in childproofing the environment as you can, but remember that nothing is a substitute for adult supervision of your child's activities. Thorough childproofing simply makes your job a bit easier. (See also Accidents (Prevention), page 7; Poisoning, page 105; and Safety Gates, page 109.)

CHOKING

Choking is the fourth most common cause of accidental death among children between the ages of one and five. The best way to deal with choking is to prevent it in the first place, because when it happens it may be too late. Face the fact that a baby or toddler is going to put anything within reach into the mouth.

Young children have been known to swallow an odd assortment of small objects which, in most cases, pass right through the digestive system. However, if an object gets into the windpipe (instead of the esophagus and digestive system) breathing can be blocked with immediately disasterous results.

The best way to keep your child from choking is to keep away from him or her anything that could cause it.

• All small objects (½ inch in diameter or less) should be completely out of reach at all times. Don't let your child play with coins, buttons, tacks, erasers, screws, or any other objects of similar size.

• Check out your child's toys to make sure that there are no small parts which could be removed. Be especially careful of things like the eyes of stuffed animals or the wheels of model cars. Even if an item looks appealing and is sold in a reliable toystore, it may not be safe. Use your own judgment. The United States Consumer Product Safety Commission does test toys and recalls particularly hazardous models. However, these procedures occur too late for some children. It's best for you to monitor carefully whatever objects your child plays with.

• Don't offer your toddler food items such as popcorn, peanuts, or raisins. These don't break apart easily but are small and light and can easily be taken into the windpipe. Many pediatricians suggest that such snacks be avoided until a child is five or six years old.

• Even some foods which would appear to be harmless and healthful could cause choking in a child who has front teeth only, but no molars to enable complete and adequate chewing. For example, celery stalks, raw carrot sticks, or apple wedges could be easily bitten into tiny pieces which could be inhaled. Save these snacks until you're sure that your toddler has the teeth, the know-how, and the discipline to chew them properly.

First Aid for Choking

What should you do if your child begins to choke? Don't waste time finding someone else to help. Seconds can be precious.

• If he or she is able to cry or speak and is breathing or coughing, it's best to do nothing. Chances are, the child will cough up the obstruction and all will be well.

• If the child can't breathe, you must do something immediately. First, if you can see what's causing the obstruction, try to remove it with a hooked index finger. If you can't, don't probe. You'll risk pushing the object farther in.

• If you are unable to remove the object, hold your child upsidedown and hit him or her sharply between the shoulder blades. This should remove the obstruction.

• If the above measures haven't worked, you'll need to try the Heimlich Maneuver. Holding the child in front of you, wrap your arms around him or her. Place one fist over the child's stomach, the other hand over the fist, and make a sudden sharp motion upward toward the chest and under the breastbone. This procedure, the most effective for adult choking victims, is best done by someone who knows how, because done wrong it can harm a child. However, at this point, you would have little choice.

You might want to ask your doctor about the first aid procedures for choking so that you are fully informed and prepared in case you ever need to use them.

If someone else is around, you attend to your child while the other person tries to summon professional help. If you succeed in removing the obstruction but the child does not begin to breathe, begin mouth-to-mouth rescue breathing immediately. (See page 34 for directions.)

CLOTHING

The clothing you get for your baby or toddler will depend on where you live and the time of year, as well as your personal preferences. There is no one "right" list of things you should have. Here are a few things to keep in mind as you plan what to buy.

• Until your child is toilet trained, you'll want to dress him or her in things which provide easy access to the diaper area.

• Remember that the things your child eats and plays with will inevitably leave their marks on the clothes, so ease of laundering is a must. If an indoor garment requires dry cleaning, it's not a wise choice for a child.

• During and after toilet training, dress your child in clothes he or she can easily remove or pull down without help. Pants should be fairly loose with a wide elastic waistband. Avoid items with complicated fasteners or garments which require complete disrobing before your child can use the toilet.

• Pajamas should be flame retardant. They must be washed according to the directions so that they won't lose this quality.

• Clothes that your toddler can learn to put on or off on his or her own are a plus for developing independence.

43

COLDS

A cold is a contagious viral infection of the membranes of the nose and throat. Contrary to popular belief, people don't catch colds from being in drafts, going out on cold or wet days, forgetting to wear a sweater or hat, or keeping the house too cool. As a matter of fact, overheated dry air indoors dries out the mucous membranes and may make a person more susceptible to colds. Colds are caused by a virus. The best way to prevent your child from getting a cold is to keep him or her away from anyone who has one.

Preschool children get more colds than any other age group. They haven't yet built up much immunity to cold viruses. Most young children get at least six colds a year. A toddler's cold often begins with a high fever which usually lasts a day or two. Common cold symptoms include stuffy or runny nose, mild sore throat, hoarseness or dry cough, watery eyes, and a general achy feeling.

Most colds can be treated at home and will go away without problem in about a week.

• If your child is too young to blow his or her nose, you can use a suction bulb (available in any pharmacy) to help clear the nasal passages.

• Your child's physician may suggest nose drops and tell you how to use them. Saline nose drops (one cup of warm water and ¼ teaspoon of salt) are effective, inexpensive, and easy to prepare.

• Antibiotics do not cure colds, so don't administer any on your own. If the cold develops complications, your child's doctor may prescribe an antibiotic to deal with the secondary infection. If so, use it as directed. (See Antibiotics, page 14.)

• More moisture in the air may make the cold sufferer more comfortable. Use a cold mist humidifier. (See Vaporizers, page 142.)

• Fluids are important. Offer your child water or juice at least once an hour—more often if he or she will take it.

• Most over-the-counter cold remedies are useless. Don't dose your child in hopes of curing the cold. Do not give aspirin to a young child with a virus cold. In extremely rare cases, the use of aspirin has been linked to Reye's Syndrome, a disease which can be fatal. (See page 108.) If your child has aches, fever, or a sore throat, and you feel you must give something, acetaminophen (e.g., Tylenol, Tempra, or Liquiprin) is a wiser choice. Ask your pediatrician.

Don't be discouraged if it seems that your child gets one cold after another. As immunity to the cold viruses builds up, the frequency of colds will decrease. Preschool children seem to pass colds from friend to friend and back again. In a few years, your child will probably have only half as many colds. There's not much you can do in the meantime.

COMFORT HABITS

Many babies develop their own little habits which they use to comfort themselves and provide a sense of security at bedtime, naptime, or times of stress. These habits usually persist through toddlerhood and, for many children, they last even longer. These personal comfort habits are generally no cause for concern. They diminish and disappear when the need is no longer there. Don't make a fuss over them.

For many children, sucking—fingers, thumb, or an object such as a pacifier—becomes a comfort habit. Some children adopt a rhythmic motion of some sort. Rocking back and forth, twirling the hair, pulling at an ear, or banging the head are different forms of rhythmic comfort habits. Your child may employ one or more of these as a relaxation technique. Severe head banging which causes pain should not be assumed to be a harmless habit without further investigation. If your child employs this extreme form of self comfort, you might try to figure out the underlying causes. (See Head Banging, page 77.)

The popular cartoon character Linus, complete with blanket, has many counterparts in real life. Many children adopt a special object to use as a "lovey" or "cuddly." For one child the precious object might be a blanket, an article of clothing, or a soft cloth. For another it might be a stuffed animal, a rag doll, or a tiny pillow. Whatever your child's choice of "lovey" might be, here are some points to keep in mind.

• Use of a cuddly object for comfort is a normal and healthy behavior for a baby or toddler. A child who uses a "lovey" for solace at bedtime is beginning to develop an independent sense of security that is under his or her control.

• Protect the precious object from loss or destruction if you can. A duplicate held for safekeeping isn't a bad idea, although it will never smell or feel quite the same. If the object is a blanket or a cloth, some parents recommend cutting it in half so that there's some left in case of an accident. This might work, but there are children who would notice. Use your judgment.

• If you travel, be sure to take the object along. A child in unfamiliar surroundings will need it more than ever.

• Continuous use of an object as a comfort habit at times other than bedtime or naptime may signal the start of a problem. If you are with your child, and there are other things to be done during the daytime, and your child persistently refuses to relinquish the object to do these other things, explore the situation further. Your child may need additional support and comfort from you to make giving up the object easier. Ask your doctor for advice if you think your child avoids other activities and relies too much on the comfort device.

CONJUNCTIVITIS (Pink Eye)

Conjunctivitis (commonly called "Pink Eye") is an irritation of the linings of the eyelids and the outside covering of the eyeballs. The eyelids may be swollen and the eyes may be weepy and red. The discharge from the eyes may form a crust which sticks the lids closed while the child sleeps.

Conjunctivitis can be highly contagious. Keep an affected child's washcloth and anything else which comes in contact with the eyes away from other members of the family. Wash your hands after touching the child. Try to keep the child from rubbing his or her eyes, although with a baby or toddler this is a seemingly impossible task.

Consult a physician if your child develops the symptoms of "Pink Eye." The treatment will vary according to the exact cause of the problem. Drops or ointment may be prescribed. Because of the highly contagious nature of the disease, you shouldn't use the same dropper or ointment on more than one member of the family. There are several possible causes of conjunctivitis, so you should avoid using last time's medicine for a new outbreak unless the doctor tells you to do so.

CONTRARINESS

Contrariness is part of a child's effort to develop independence, and it is an inevitable characteristic of toddlerhood. At some point during your child's second year, "NO!" is likely to become a highly favored word and cause you considerable frustration. You'll probably find it easier to cope with your child at this stage if you approach the contrariness with cleverness rather than as an invitation to combat. Here are some specific suggestions.

• Make cooperation fun whenever possible. For example, instead of issuing an order to pick up the toys, try making a game of it. "Let's see who can put the things away faster—you or Daddy." Having the child pick up two items while you pick up five or six is certainly preferable to a situation in which no one picks up any or you do them all in anger.

• Keep in mind that a toddler who says "No," doesn't always mean it but may simply be saying it on general principles. Tactfully arrange for your child to be able to change his or her mind without losing face.

• Warn your child when you're going to make a demand that is likely to provoke contrariness. For example, say "In five minutes you'll have to wash your hands and get ready for lunch." Or, "When this program is over we're going to turn off the television and go outside." This enables you to build into your demand a small bit of time for a child to be defiant and get it out of his or her system before doing what you wanted in the first place.

• Avoid elaborate explanations in your efforts to enlist cooperation. Keep your requests and your reasons simple and to the point. There are times when all the reason you need offer a toddler is "Because I want you to do it." It's possible, however, for you to maintain control without being mean or confronting, and this is what you should aim for.

• Whenever possible, give your child choices between desirable alternatives. This leaves you in control, but gives the child a chance to express independence. For example, "Which sweater do you want to put on —your blue one or your green one?" is less likely to stir up a battle than "Put on your sweater."

• Keep in mind that a family is not a democracy in which the demands and desires of a toddler should have equal weight with the decisions of the parents. It's important to let your child try to be independent in ways that are appropriate, but you must not relinquish control in areas which would compromise your child's safety or the well being of the rest of the family. For example, encourage your child to feed or dress himself or herself as much as possible. Don't, however, permit that same child to decide to play with dangerous objects or ride unrestrained in the car to find out what it's like without a car seat.

• Don't argue. There will be times when you must enforce your wishes against your child's will. Do it calmly, kindly, and firmly. Say, "I know you'd rather stay outside (or whatever), but now we're going to . . ." Then pick up your child and get on with it. These times will be less frequent and less upsetting if you act in a matter-of-fact way and avoid anger.

No matter how beautifully you manage to cope with your child's contrariness, there still may be days when nothing goes right. Try not to lose your cool. Remember that the contrary stage, although very difficult at times, doesn't last forever. Your child will soon become more competent in language and other activities and the contrariness will give way to cooperation as the desire to imitate adult behavior becomes stronger than the desire to defy you. Contrariness as a way of life will reappear when your child becomes an adolescent, but in the meantime you'll have a few years respite.

CONVULSIONS (Seizures)

Convulsions in a young child are a frightening experience for the parents but these seizures generally pass without lasting harm. A convulsion is caused by irritation to the brain. This often accompanies high fever. Some children are more susceptible than others to convulsions. If your child tends toward feverish seizures, your child's pediatrician will advise you on steps to take to keep fever as low as possible whenever your child is ill. (See Fever, page 72).

If your child has a seizure (convulsions) here's what to do:

(1) Put the child on his or her abdomen or side on a surface where the thrashing about won't cause injury. A carpet will do nicely. A bed is O.K. as long as you make sure the child doesn't fall off the edge.

(2) If you can, loosen the child's clothing, especially anything around the neck.

(3) Look at a clock to note the time. Observe carefully what is happening so you will be able to describe it to the doctor.

(4) Let the seizure carry on as it will, and don't try to hold the child still. When it's over, put the child on his or her side, with the head slightly lower than the rest of the body.

(5) At no time during or right after a convulsion should you give the child anything by mouth. Don't try to force the jaws apart or use any object to hold the mouth open.

(6) If the seizure lasts longer than 15-20 minutes, get help and proceed to the nearest hospital as fast as you can. Prolonged seizures (45-60 minutes) may result in lasting damage.

If you are alone, tend to your child first and call the doctor as soon as the seizure has passed. If someone is with you, have that person call the doctor while you take care of the child.

If your child seems to have a tendency toward convulsions, your pediatrician may recommend further testing to make sure that the seizures are fever-related and not due to a more serious problem such as epilepsy.

CREEPING AND CRAWLING

Some time around six months of age or a bit later a baby is likely to figure out a way to get about without being carried. When this happens, life with your child becomes more interesting and considerably more demanding. You can no longer count on your child to remain quietly where he or she is put.

Different children devise different techniques of locomotion. Watch your child carefully. You'll probably be quite fascinated at the way he or she develops into a mobile baby. Some of the methods of moving about look quite comical. Some children push along on the stomach long before they can support themselves on hands and knees. Many children begin their creeping by moving backwards which seems to be easier. Children who can sit often learn how to move along in a sitting position with a hand behind to push and a leg stretched out to pull.

True crawling—supporting oneself on hands and knees and moving the arms and legs in some coordinated way to cover distance—usually takes a while longer to develop. Some babies have it worked out by eight months. Others take till a year or longer to crawl efficiently. A few seem to skip the crawling stage almost entirely and go right to upright locomotion holding onto pieces of furniture. Some babies get the crawling position right but take days or even weeks to figure out how to move the arms and legs in a way that propels them forward.

Whatever way your child develops to move about, perhaps the most important task for you is to reevaluate your house for potential hazards. Try to view the world from your baby's vantage point, less than a foot above floor level. Here are some of the precautions you must take to protect your mobile baby.

• Keep your baby off the stairs by installing gates at the top and the bottom. Use gates to keep your child out of certain rooms if you wish.

48

• Place safety caps in all unused electric outlets or cover them securely with tape so that your child can't poke things into them.

• When your child is on the floor, make sure that all lamps and small appliances are unplugged to prevent the baby from pulling things down on his or her head.

• Make sure the floor is reasonably clean and free of all tiny objects that could be swallowed.

• Install childproof latches on all low cabinets. It's best to store dangerous substances (cleaning materials, etc.) in cabinets that are completely out of reach.

• Keep breakable objects out of reach, both for the sake of the objects and for your child.

When your baby becomes mobile your new responsibilities will take some getting used to. The child can be literally under your feet one moment and seconds later can be in another room getting into trouble. Some children are more difficult to handle than others, but a good rule to follow is never to trust a mobile baby who has crawled out of your sight.

CROUP

Croup is a type of laryngitis which for a baby or toddler, whose breathing passages are still very small, can be an emergency requiring immediate help. Croup can be a very frightening experience for the parents as well as the sick child.

An attack of croup usually occurs at night, when the child coughs, wakes, tries to cry, and has difficulty breathing. A child with croup sounds somewhat like a cross between a strangling crow and a barking puppy.

If your child has an attack of croup, what should you do? Have someone else call the doctor, if possible, while you attend to the child. Here's what to do unless your doctor directs otherwise.

(1) Turn on the hot taps in the bathroom (especially the shower) so that the room becomes steamy as fast as possible. Use an electric teakettle in a small room if you don't have hot running water. While waiting for the room to steam up, try step two.

(2) A few breaths of cold air may help reduce the swelling of the larynx. Hold the child at the window for five or six breaths of night air. Or, open the freezer door long enough for the child (warmly wrapped) to breath a minute of cold moist air.

(3) Spend about ten to fifteen minutes holding your child in an upright position in the steamy bathroom or other room you've prepared. This should relieve the breathing problems.

(4) Although this is easier said than done, try to keep the child calm. A relaxed child needs less oxygen than one who's in a panic.

When the worst of the attack seems to have passed, you can deal with getting the child to medical help. If you have not been able to reach the doctor, don't hesitate to take your child to the nearest emergency room. If you have reached the doctor, do what he or she directs. The doctor may want you to bring the child to the hospital by car or ambulance. Or you may be advised to continue the moisture in the air at home for a while (see Vaporizers, page 142).

The first attack of croup is likely to be the most upsetting, because you won't be prepared for it. If your child seems to have a tendency toward this problem, your doctor will advise you of what to do to minmize the chances of a severe attack. It may be necessary to provide extra moisture in the air throughout the winter months or at least any time your child shows signs of a cold.

CURIOSITY

Curiosity is a vital characteristic of a young child. Curiosity will keep your child very busy. This has its drawbacks, but it is an important part of learning. Keep your child safe, but try not to stamp out the curiosity and inclination to explore. A curious child is not being naughty, but is doing what comes naturally.

The strong curiosity of a newly mobile baby or toddler is not matched by manual dexterity or understanding of cause and effect. You must keep from the child's reach any substance which could cause harm. (See Accidents (Prevention), page 7.) You'll also want to remove from reach any object which could be damaged by a curious child. Remember that it's curiosity, not

badness which causes a child to head for the crystal vase on the coffee table. And, if the vase should meet the floor and smash, count yourself as the naughty one. It's unreasonable to expect a baby or toddler to act contrary to nature and stay away from enticing objects. As language and understanding develop, you can teach that kind of self-discipline, but it takes time, patience, and longer than the toddler years. Crystal vases are not a good item on which to practice.

As your child grows, the physical capacity to follow where curiosity leads will increase. No longer confined to crawling, the child can walk, run, and climb. Good judgment does not develop at the same pace, so unless carefully supervised, a toddler's self-initiated exploring and learning activities can lead to trouble.

50

Many young children enjoy hearing the popular stories about Curious George. Most of the Curious George books are available in paperback. Don't count on your toddler, however, to make the direct connection between Curious George getting into trouble and what could happen to a curious toddler in your own home. There are lessons to be learned from these books but keeping the crystal vases and dangerous substances out of reach is still safer for all until you are absolutely certain that these lessons have been learned.

DAWDLING

Dawdling is an absolutely normal and characteristic toddler behavior. The fact that dawdling is normal, however, makes it no less exasperating to caregivers. Nevertheless, it's best not to let your exasperation escalate into combat with a child who is simply doing what toddlers do. Try to understand why a toddler dawdles and come up with coping strategies to minimize the conflict.

• Allow more time for what once seemed like simple daily routines. Face the fact that hurrying generally isn't a toddler's style. Leave lots of time for bathing, getting dressed, cleaning up the clutter, getting out of the house, shopping, and similar activities. Things are going to happen slowly when a two-year-old is "helping" you. If you leave enough time for things to take longer, you won't be as irritated when they *do* take longer.

• If you don't have the luxury of extra time to allow for routine tasks, plan in advance the best way to manage without a hassle in the time available. For example, if you don't have much time for shopping, drive to the store or take public transportation and keep your child in a shopping cart or stroller. This is preferable to trying to make your child walk as fast as you would like to. If dawdling in the bath is a problem, set a timer and gently but firmly remove your child from the tub when the bell rings. If an activity is dragging on too long, take matters into your own hands and get on with something else *before* you get angry. Diversion is an excellent management device.

• Some of a toddler's slowness is simply an inability to cover as much ground as an adult can. Little short legs must take several steps to every one of yours. If you're in a hurry, don't depend on your child to keep up. Use a stroller.

• Understand that some dawdling may be a mild form of contrariness as a toddler is learning to be independent. Taking his or her own sweet time about something is one way a toddler can learn to exert some control over what's going on. This can be a valuable learning experience. If it is inconvenient to permit such a learning experience at a particular time, don't feel guilty about intervening and pulling rank. Just avoid getting angry, which would only make matters worse. Change the scene or the activity, but don't blame the child for being a toddler.

• Take the time to enjoy some dawdling along with your child. Seeing the world through a toddler's eyes can be a refreshing and wonderful experience. A toddler doesn't have a clear concept of what time is all about. *Now* is the most meaningful to a toddler, who doesn't worry about the future or fret about the past nearly as much as adults do. When was the last time you stopped to sniff or look closely at a flower, to examine a leaf, a bug, or even a spot on the sidewalk? Everything is so fresh and new to a toddler that hurrying along isn't nearly as enticing as exploring along the way. Try to share experiences with your child. You'll both benefit.

DAY CARE

If yours is a single parent family or both parents work outside the home, appropriate day-care arrangements for your preschool child must be made. How you choose to handle day care will depend, of course, on what facilities are available in your area as well as on what you can afford to pay.

A caregiver who comes to your own home on a regular basis is likely to be the most flexible in terms of scheduling and procedures, as well as the most expensive. An alternative to day care in your own home is day care for your child in someone else's home. You may be able to find a family near you which takes one or more children on a regular basis for day care. Or, you might choose a professionally staffed day-care center which may or may not be affiliated with an agency (e.g. community center, religious group, educational organization) and which may or may not be licensed.

Before selecting a day-care situation for your child, visit the available choices *with your child.* Schedule your visit during caregiving hours so you can see what goes on there. Look around and listen. Observe how the children interact with each other and with the caregiver(s). See how your child responds, but don't let your decision be strongly influenced in a negative way if your child prefers staying with you to entering into the activities. You may have to settle for the feeling that your child would participate in such a place if he or she got used to it.

Discuss with the caregiver(s) topics of importance to you. Don't be afraid to ask questions. Try to phrase your questions so they promote conversation rather than simple "Yes" or "No" answers. Among the subjects you might bring up are books for children, available toys and activities, formal instruction (if any) such as reading readiness, use of pacifiers, toilet training, discipline, aggressive behavior, television, policy regarding sick children, staffing, feeding, and anything else of importance to you. While there may be no one right or wrong view on any or all of these topics, finding out how the views of the caregiver(s) compare to your own can help you evaluate the suitability of the facility for your child.

When you've found out as much as you can, it's probably soundest to go with your instincts. How you feel about a place is as good a way to choose as any, as long as these feelings are based on observations and information.

DEATH

Death is a difficult matter for most people to discuss. How should you explain death to a young child? There really isn't any "best way," and you should do what's consistent with your family's beliefs. Answer a child's questions honestly and sincerely, and don't make up stories you'll have to undo later. By the age of two, many children will be able to grasp some notion of what death means although the permanence of death will not be understood. And even a younger child will notice the absence of a significant person although the reason for the absence may be beyond comprehension at that time.

Questions About Death

A young child may hear about someone dying and ask you what it means to "die." Your answer should be simple and direct. If you believe in a life beyond this world, you'll probably find it easier to talk about death in a religious context. You certainly can tell your child, "A person who dies goes to heaven to be with God," if that's what you believe. If you don't believe in an afterlife, you can tell a child that to die means to stop being alive. Don't describe death as "going to sleep," however, or you may create bedtime fears and problems. Avoid talking about death as "going away" because that expression may lead a child to worry when you go away even for a short time.

If a child asks, "Am I going to die?" try to be truthful in a way that won't cause fears. You can say that everyone will die someday but that most people die when they are very old, or very sick, or if they get very badly hurt. Reassure your child that you don't expect that to happen, and that you expect him or her and yourself to be around for a long long time.

Death of a Pet

The death of a pet is often the first experience a child has with death. Even if you're secretly glad to have one less animal around, don't let those feelings show if you can help it. Permit your child to be sad and to engage in appropriate rituals to accompany the death of a pet. This can be an important learning experience.

Don't flush the goldfish down the toilet or toss the deceased cat out with the trash and hope your toddler won't notice. The child *will* notice and his or her trust in you is likely to be shaken. A simple burial for a beloved pet will help your child deal with the reality of the loss as well as demonstrate a reverence and respect for life. If a child wants to add a departed animal to the list of "God bless _____" at bedtime, such remembrance will do no harm.

An excellent book for very young children is *The Tenth Good Thing About Barney,* by Judith Viorst (Atheneum, New York: 1971). The story is about a little boy whose cat, Barney, has died. This book, useful to help a child cope with the death of a pet, is worth sharing at any time.

Death of a Loved One

If a person close to a young child dies—a parent, grandparent or other relative, or even a neighbor or family friend—the child will be faced with dealing both with the loss of the person and with the grief and preoccupation of those who remain. This can be very frightening to a child.

If someone dies and you are grieving, be honest with your child. Admit that you are sad because someone dear to you has died. Reassure the child that he or she was not in any way the cause of the death. Explain the death in religious terms if this fits in with your beliefs.

Should you take a young child to a funeral? That depends. Make whatever decision seems to make the most sense to you in the particular situation. If your child is old enough to understand, and the person who died was very close, going to the funeral might be a meaningful experience as long as you are able to provide the child with comfort and support. Don't force a child to go if he or she doesn't want to. Follow your instincts.

A book which deals in a sympathetic and sensitive way with a child's grief and the death of a loved one is *My Grandpa Died Today*, by Joan Fassler (Human Sciences Press, New York: 1971). The book is intended for school age children, but the text and illustrations might help you find the words for talking to a younger child about the death of an elderly person. An excellent story to read directly to your toddler is the last one in the collection *Stories From a Snowy Meadow*, by Carla Stevens (Houghton Mifflin, Boston: 1976).

DENTAL CARE

Before your child begins kindergarten, or sooner if you suspect any problems, it's time for his or her first visit to the dentist. From then on, visits twice a year are recommended. It's important to take good care of your child's baby teeth even though they will be replaced by permanent ones later. Even in baby teeth, cavities should be filled because tooth decay can cause painful toothaches and the premature loss of a baby tooth can cause the position of the remaining teeth to shift. Regular visits to the dentist can help keep potential problems under control.

For most people, going to the dentist will never rate as one of life's preferred activities, and there's no point in making it any worse for your child than necessary. A pedodontist is a dentist who specializes in the care and treatment of children's teeth. If you can find one near you, this might be a good choice for the early years.

Daily care of the teeth (even if there are only a few of them) should include brushing after meals with a soft-bristled brush and a pleasant-tasting fluoride toothpaste. Your child will probably enjoy imitating you with the toothbrush, but it's best if you help him or her do the job at least once a day to make sure that no important places are missed. If brushing after eating is impossible, a drink of water will help.

Avoid the practice of letting your child drink heavily sweetened fruit drinks (especially from a nursing bottle). A nighttime bottle of milk or juice might soothe your child to sleep, but it will also leave decay-causing substances between the teeth and should be avoided. (See Candy and Sweets, page 35.)

DIAPERING (Choices)

By the time you and your baby are ready for the suggestions in this book, you've probably already changed hundreds—perhaps thousands—of diapers. If you originally decided on cloth diapers for economic and/or ecological reasons, and that decision has worked out well for you, then there's no reason to change what you are doing. If, however, you find yourself drowning in laundry and you feel the time you spend with cloth diapers could better be spent enjoying your baby, don't feel guilty about changing to disposables.

If your reasons for choosing cloth diapers were ecological (the plastic coverings of disposables are not biodegradable and the paper parts are made from trees), remember that laundering of cloth diapers adds detergent wastes to the environment and that a washer and dryer consume energy. If your reasons for choosing cloth diapers were economic, be sure to add in the costs of doing laundry (detergent, hot water, electricity) and a reasonable compensation for your own time before you decide for sure that cloth diapers are cheaper.

Try different brands of disposables until you find which ones work best for you and your baby. As your baby grows and changes shape, you might find a change in brand as well as size to be helpful. The diaper that fit beautifully and did the job just right up until two weeks ago may not be the best choice now. If you are experimenting with sizes or brands, be sure to buy the small box. This way a mistake will not be too expensive. When you've found the type that suits your baby best, it's most economical to buy the larger convenience packs or cases. Shop for price, which can vary considerably from one store to another.

DIAPERING (Techniques)

Diapering a newborn is relatively easy. The "how-to" pictures on the disposable diaper box are an excellent guide. Lift the child by the feet, remove the dirty diaper, clean the small bottom, and put on the new diaper. There's nothing to it. As soon as a baby becomes the slightest bit mobile, however, this once simple procedure can become a conflict if you're not clever about it.

What should you do when your child begins to add variety to every diaper change by rolling, wriggling, or scooting along on the changing surface? An interesting object thrust into little hands may divert attention long enough to let you finish the change. This strategy works better than force. Talk to your child as you change the diaper. Describe each step as you do it, but get it done as fast as you can.

If you use disposables, try to get the tapes on somehow— even if your child moves the wrong way just at the stickiest moment. Then, if necessary, make adjustments and repair the damage with masking tape. Once the diaper is sort of on, it's easier to straighten it, one side at a time. If you use pins, a bar of soap keeps the points slippery and provides a good storage place for extras. (Store out of your child's reach, and count the ones you use at each change. If you take two pins out, put two back in!)

Few, if any, toddlers lie still for a diaper change. You'll quickly become skilled at removing and applying diapers to a standing child who may even be trying to walk or run somewhere as you do the job. As with rolling babies, an interesting object to hold might help. Try, if you wish, to enlist your toddler's cooperation with the various steps of the changing procedure. Let him or her help you pull the pants down, remove the old diaper, and fasten the new. The corner of a room is a good place to change a diaper on a toddler, because there's no place for the child to go until you're done with it. Occasionally a toddler will be willing to play "baby" and lie down nicely. This game doesn't work often enough to be used as a regular strategy, but on rare occasions it can provide a bit of nostalgia along with an easy diaper change.

DIAPER RASH

Diaper rash can be very painful. To help prevent diaper rash, change the diaper frequently and wash the child's bottom at *every* change. Here are some suggestions to follow if your child shows any signs of diaper rash.

• Clean the diaper area with water or disposable wipes after every change. Do this even if the diaper is wet rather than soiled. (The ammonia left by the urine can be extremely irritating to tender skin even if the child looks clean.)

• Change the diaper more often. This is especially important if you use disposable diapers which can hold a lot of irritating moisture without seeming to be wet.

• If you use cloth diapers, skip the rubber pants for a while. Use two diapers at once to prevent leaks.

• If you can, try letting the child go without any diaper at all for a while. Exposure to air helps stop the rash. Put several layers of diaper and a rubber pad under the child to protect the crib.

• If your location and the time of year permit, a little sunshine and fresh air can be a help. But be careful not to trade diaper rash for a sunburned bottom!

• An ointment such as Vaseline, A & D, Desitin, or Diaperene may help protect your child's bottom from diaper rash and give healing a chance to start if a rash has started. Zinc oxide ointment is inexpensive and effective.

• If you use cloth diapers, make sure that they are well rinsed so no soap remains. Changing brands of detergent or using a liquid detergent may help. Raise the temperature of the wash water if possible. A softener might help. A cup of white vinegar in the rinse water will neutralize traces of ammonia from the baby's urine. After laundering diapers, you can boil them for ten minutes or so in a great big pot of water. This is an extra precaution to make sure that the irritants have been removed. In good weather, sun drying and bleaching are the best possible neutralizers. If cloth diapers still appear soiled or grayish after careful laundering, it's all right to use bleach. Be sure to rinse very thoroughly. Stained diapers definitely seem to increase the risk of getting a persistent diaper rash.

If you've tried these suggestions for two or three days and your child has a severe diaper rash which does not seem to respond to treatment, consult your physician.

DISCIPLINE

Everyone needs discipline, which is a structure or set of rules for behavior. To provide effective discipline for a baby or toddler, it's best to arrange the environment (childproof it) so that the child doesn't have constant opportunity to do things which are dangerous or naughty. It's important for a child's wellbeing to have predictable limits set on his or her behavior, and to have these limits enforced. Your child may continually test the limits you set, and his or her sense of security in part depends on those limits being there despite protests.

A young child is usually incapable of thinking through the consequences of behavior, understanding cause and effect relationships, or understanding elaborate sets of verbal instructions. So, the first steps in providing discipline must involve stacking the deck in your favor by arranging things so that it's easier for your child to do what you want, and difficult to do otherwise.

When—despite your best efforts at prevention—a mobile baby or toddler gets into something you wish he or she hadn't, remove the child physically from the situation. This is not the time for attempts to reason with the child, lengthy verbal requests and explanations, or lack of firmness. Removing the child from the problem is generally the best form of discipline. Keep your comments brief and to the point. There's no point in launching into a lecture that's beyond the child's ability to comprehend.

As you provide structure for your child, it's important not to confuse discipline with punishment. Punishment is the penalty for breaking the rules, and until your child is old enough to understand the rules and relate breaking them to the consequences, punishment is almost always an inappropriate way to manage the child's behavior. (See Punishment, page 107; Child Abuse, page 39; and Contrariness, page 46.)

> A book to help you provide appropriate limits and discipline for your children is *Parent Power: A Common-Sense Approach to Raising Children in the Eighties,* by John K. Rosemond (East Woods Press, Charlotte, NC: 1981). Written in an interesting and witty style, this volume—true to its title's promise—is full of common sense and practical advice for parents.

DISEASES (Common Childhood)

Because of widespread and effective immunization programs, your child will be spared most of the common childhood diseases that were virtually inevitable two or three generations ago. The use of antibiotics has made some diseases such as strep throat and scarlet fever far less serious than these illnesses were in the past.

During the regular well-child visits to the doctor or clinic, your child will be protected against measles, mumps, rubella (German measles), pertussis (whooping cough), diphtheria, tetanus, and polio. Routine smallpox vaccination is no longer recommended because this disease has been successfully eliminated from the United States.

Many children still get chicken pox, for which there is not yet a vaccine approved for general use. If your child contracts chicken pox, your doctor will advise you on specific treatment. The childhood disease your child is most likely to get—over and over again—is the common cold. (See Colds, page 44.) Although vaccines for influenza viruses are available, young children are not usually given "flu shots" unless there is some other medical reason a bout with influenza would be especially hazardous.

DIVORCE

If divorce becomes part of your family situation during your child's early years, try to minimize its negative impact. Make whatever decisions you must, however, and don't try to live in an impossible situation "for the children's sake."

• Reassure your child that his or her needs will still be met even though both parents will no longer be living together. Then make every effort to keep your word.

• Try not to communicate to your child any bitterness or hostility you might have for your partner. Permit the child to retain whatever pleasant feeling he or she may have for the other parent no matter what *your* feelings might be.

• Don't burden a toddler with specific details of adult problems, but be careful to reassure your child that he or she is in no way to blame for the breakup.

DOCTORS

The choice of a doctor — pediatrician or family practitioner — to meet your child's health care needs should be made very carefully. During the years your child is growing up, you will be likely to have many dealings with this person. It's important for you to have confidence in the doctor's professional competence. It's equally important that you feel able to communicate comfortably with him or her. You should share similar philosophies of child rearing.

The material that follows is designed to help you select the right physician for your child. If you already have a pediatrician for your family or, if your geographic area provides few alternatives, you probably shouldn't take much time with this section. You might, however, find this material useful to remind you of questions to ask or issues you might like to handle in a different way than you have in the past.

In selecting a pediatrician, you may find it helpful to meet with one or two, or more until you find the right one. Many doctors charge for this consultation. Others don't. Either way, it's time or money well spent.

Finding Pediatricians

Here are some sources of possible candidates.

• Ask your obstetrician for the names of pediatricians who would suit your personal style as well as your child's needs. Call the nearest hospital and ask for a list of pediatricians who are attending physicians on the hospital staff.

• A La Leche League leader in your area could identify pediatricians who are especially supportive to nursing mothers.

Things to Find Out

• What can you find out about the doctor's training and special qualifications? What are his or her hospital affiliations? Do they include the hospital where you would be most likely to take your child in an emergency? (It's best if the answer to this question is yes.)

• Where is the doctor's office located? Is it convenient? How would you get there? Could you get there easily in an emergency?

Additional Questions

There are no "right" or "wrong" answers to these questions, but you might have preferences which you should think about in advance rather than being unhappy later.

• Would you prefer a young, recently trained doctor or an older, more experienced one? Or, doesn't it matter to you?

• Would you prefer your child's doctor to be a man or a woman, or don't you care about this? (Keep in mind that you are selecting a medical specialist, not a substitute mother or father for your child.) If you feel strongly, however, that you would communicate better with a woman (or man), then by all means try to find a suitable pediatrician of the preferred sex.

• Would you prefer a group practice or a pediatrician who practices alone? If you select a group, will you be able to make appointments (except in an emergency) with the doctor of your choice? Or, will your child see more than one doctor on a rotating basis? If you choose a doctor who practices alone, how are emergencies covered in his or her absence?

The Pediatrician's Office

• When you call the office for a consultation appointment, how are you treated? While you are in the waiting room, notice how other incoming calls are handled.

• What goes on in the doctor's waiting room? Is it pleasant and furnished with children in mind? Does the doctor appear to be hopelessly behind schedule? If so, is this typical? Are you treated courteously? While it may not be completely fair to judge a doctor by the office, in most cases it's reasonable to assume that the staff and the surroundings reflect the doctor's attitude and approach.

• What are the fees? How do they compare to those of other doctors in your area? What payment terms are required? (The most expensive doctor is not necessarily the best. One with bargain rates may not be the best choice either.)

Meeting the Doctor

Here are some topics to discuss when you meet with the doctor. If you have strong personal views on any of these issues, it's best to pick a doctor with whom you agree, or at least one who's neutral and flexible.

• What are the doctor's views on bottle- vs. breast-feeding? Will he or she support you in *your* choice? A nursing mother needs support and encouragement, not a doctor who orders supplements or a complete switch to bottles at the first sign of difficulty. A woman who prefers to bottle-feed doesn't need a pediatrician who makes her feel guilty about this.

• When does the doctor generally recommend that a baby begin solid foods? A very early introduction to solids may indicate less than total commitment to breast-feeding. A doctor who makes the decision for each child according to special needs may be more flexible than one who starts all children of a certain age on solid foods.

• How does the doctor's office handle telephone questions about your baby's health and care? Is there a telephone hour each morning when you can speak to the doctor directly? Or, does the office take calls all day and have the doctor get back to you as soon as possible. (Either method is O.K. as long as you feel your requests for information will be answered.)

• What role does the doctor's staff play? Will routine questions be answered by a nurse or assistant? This may be a plus. The doctor who is frequently tied up on the telephone answering routine questions about shampoo or brands of babyfood will be less available to deal with important medical problems of your child and others.

• What is the doctor's view on the use of pacifiers? If this opinion differs from your own, will he or she support you in your approach?

Things to Tell the Doctor

• If there are any special things about you and your family that a pediatrician should know, this is the time to bring them up. Is your family medical history of interest? Allergies? Blood type? Any history of genetic disorders?

• Are there any cultural or religious practices and beliefs in your family that relate to health care? Are there any medical procedures you would choose to refuse for your child? Do you have any special dietary practices? If you feel strongly about any controversial health care issues, it's best to find a pediatrician with whom you can discuss these things comfortably.

• Discuss your expectations with the doctor. Is he or she able and willing to provide guidance in the way that's best for your style of parenting? (Some people want a directive, authoritarian approach that spells out details and orders that they be done in a certain way. Other parents prefer general guidelines within which they can work out routines to suit themselves.) Be sure you choose a doctor whose style meets your needs.

Do you really have to go through all this to find the right doctor for your child? Perhaps not. A good recommendation or your own gut feeling when you first meet the doctor may be all the convincing you need. If you are able to work out a good relationship with a pediatrician for your child with less effort, consider yourself fortunate.

Sick Calls

When your child is sick and you call the doctor, it's best to have certain information at hand so that you can answer the doctor's questions accurately. In many offices the nurse will take the information and have the doctor call you back. Before calling, observe your child and note any symptoms you should mention. Take your child's temperature and tell the doctor exactly what it is and the method (rectal or axillary) you used to obtain it. Among the other symptoms you should mention if you observe any of them are loss of energy or appetite, vomiting, breathing difficulty, coughing, discharge from the ears or eyes, blood or mucus in the stools, excessive perspiration, signs of dehydration (lack of tears, saliva, decreased urinary output), evidence of pain. If the child does not look or act like himself or herself, mention that to the doctor. Be able to tell the doctor approximately how long you have noticed each of the symptoms.

The more information you have at your fingertips when you make the call, the better the doctor or his staff will be able to help you quickly. Make a list and don't depend on being able to remember the important details on the spot. Of course, this advice pertains to ordinary sick calls only. If your child is in an emergency or life threatening situation, don't waste time trying to make lists or take the child's temperature. Call for help immediately.

Well-Child Visits

During your child's early years, a regular schedule of "well-child" healthcare checkups will ensure that he or she receives all required immunizations and that development is going along as expected. During well-child visits to the doctor, any potential problem can be identified and watched and treatment started if necessary. A regularly followed program of preventive medical care can help minimize the need for "sick calls" to your child's physician.

A well-child visit to a physician or clinic during the first three years will usually include the following:

—questions about your child's health since the last visit (health profile)
—a physical examination
—measurements of height, weight, and (during the first year) head circumference
—a blood test and urinalysis once each year
—vision and hearing screening
—assessment of developmental level and behavior
—any required immunizations
—a chance for you to discuss with the doctor any questions or concerns you may have about your child's health

To make sure that you remember to ask the doctor about matters that concern you, bring along a list of questions. This will enable you to cover everything without unnecessarily prolonging the visit.

Work with your child's physician and don't be afraid or embarrassed to ask questions if you are worried about something or if you don't fully understand the instructions he or she is giving you. If you find, however, that despite your best efforts you are consistently unable to communicate with the professionals you have chosen for your child's health care, it might be best for all concerned if you made a change.

Well-child visits to a physician or clinic are typically scheduled within the first month after birth, and again when your child is two, four, six, nine, and twelve months of age. During the second year, visits at fifteen and eighteen months and at two years of age are recommended. If all is going well, the next regular visit can be around the time of your child's third birthday. This schedule might be modified by your physician if there is some reason to see your child at other times.

EARS (Care of)

The ears of a baby or toddler require no special care unless you suspect a problem. If so, you should consult your child's pediatrician for advice.

Ear infections are common among children, and a very young child may not be able to communicate clearly to you just where it hurts. You might suspect an earache if your child seems unusually cranky, feverish, and is pulling at or touching the side of the face. Before a child is old enough to use language effectively, ear pain is sometimes confused with teething pain. If the area about the ear seems tender or warm, or if you note a bloody or other discharge, call the doctor. It's best to treat an ear infection with the correct medication as soon as possible. If you have any doubts about whether or not your child has an ear infection, it's better to ask the doctor than to wait and see what might happen.

If your child puts an object into the ear, don't try to remove it on your own unless you're sure you can do so without making the problem worse. Something soft that can be grabbed easily with tweezers is worth a try. Wedged-in beads, beans, and similar objects are best left to the experts, and a call to the doctor or trip to the emergency room is in order.

As far as cleanliness of the ears is concerned, wash what you can see and leave it at that. Don't poke cotton-tipped swabs into the ears or dig around to remove the wax. (See also Hearing (Problems), page 78.)

ECZEMA

Eczema is an allergic reaction in which the skin becomes dry and scaly and extremely itchy. Eczema tends to run in allergy prone families, and it is most common in children under three.

If your child develops eczema, work with your pediatrician to try to identify the specific cause. Think about any recent change in the child's diet that might have triggered the attack. (For example, if the first eczema attack coincided with weaning from breast milk, suspect an allergy to cow's milk. In such cases a switch to soy bean formula is often helpful.) Think about any new substances that might have touched your child's skin and set off a problem. (For example, did you change brands of disposable diapers or switch to a new bed cover?) The answers to questions like these can help your pediatrician track down the cause of the reaction.

Here are some suggestions to make a child with eczema more comfortable.

• Because soap and water may make the situation worse, skip as many baths as possible. Use baby oil or lotion for cleansing your child's skin. Ask your doctor to recommend a bath soap for use when you do bathe your child.

• Avoid dressing your child with clothes that irritate. For example, skip the scratchy sweater and use several smooth layers instead for warmth.

• Use a vaporizer to add moisture to the air.

• Keep the child's fingernails very clean and cut short, so that his or her scratching doesn't make matters worse.

• Try to keep the child busy and diverted from the discomfort as much as possible. Make every effort to avoid adding further stress to an already unpleasant situation.

• For severe cases, the doctor may prescribe an ointment containing cortisone to reduce the discomfort. Ask. Don't medicate your child without a physician's direction.

ELECTRICAL SHOCK

A child who pokes at a live electric socket, chews a plugged-in appliance cord, or otherwise comes in contact with a live electric connection may become part of the electrical circuit. This can be a life threatening emergency. If possible, turn off the power source at once by removing the appropriate fuse or tripping the circuit breaker. If you can't do that, separate the child from the circuit, but DO NOT USE your bare hands. If you touch the child directly, you too will be shocked. Touch and move the child only with dry things that won't conduct electricity—rubber gloves or boots, a wooden chair, a broom handle, a cushion or pillow, large wooden spoons, or a rubber spatula. If the child isn't breathing, begin mouth to mouth resuscitation (rescue breathing) immediately. (See page 34.) Get medical help without delay.

EYE DROPS

If your child's physician prescribes eyedrops or ointment for any reason, here are some suggestions to help you get the medication where it belongs.

(1) Place the child on his or her back across your lap. Place one arm (your left if you are right-handed) around the back of the child's head, and reach around to the child's eye with this hand. Hold the eyelids open with your fingers.

(2) Hold the dropper with the correct dose of medication in your other hand, an inch or two above the child's eye. When the child blinks, squeeze the dropper and release the medication into the inner corner of the eye. If you squeeze when the child blinks, the drop will reach the eye just as it opens again.

For a young child, medication in ointment form may be easier to administer. Hold the child the same way as for drops. Apply the ointment to the inner corner of the eye. The child's blinking will help spread it.

EYES (care of)

Under normal circumstances, the eyes need no special care. If necessary, the lids may be gently cleansed with a cotton ball dipped in plain water. Use a fresh piece of cotton for each eye and wash from the inside corner out.

Injuries to the Eye

• Any injury to the eyeball should receive immediate medical attention. Skip home remedies and call the doctor or take your child to the emergency room. A clean, loose bandage over the eye while you're in transit may help prevent further injury and keep the child's hands off it.

• A bit of soap or shampoo in the eye will cause discomfort and perhaps some redness but no real harm. A little rinse with plain water is all that's needed. Try to keep the child from rubbing the eye.

• Any other household chemicals—cleaners, detergents, deodorants, window sprays, aerosol cleaners or polishes, etc.—should be treated as a potentially serious problem. If your child gets one of these in the eyes, flush immediately with lots of plain water. This won't be easy, but it's necessary. Turn on the tap and gently pour water into the eyes again and again from a cup or a glass. If only one eye is affected, hold the child so you don't wash the harmful substance into the other eye. Don't worry about the mess you're making. Your child's sight is far more important than a dry floor. Continue to pour the water until you are absolutely sure that no trace of the chemical remains. Ten minutes is probably enough.

• A foreign body such as dirt, sand, or an insect in the eye may well wash itself out if the child cries. Gently pulling the top lid down over the lower lid may stimulate tears. If not, you may be able to lick the particle out. This is safer than poking at the eye with a tissue or handkerchief. Hold your child's head in your hands and use your thumbs to hold the eyelids apart. Use the moist tip of your tongue to wipe over the eyeball. Chances are, this will remove the problem. If not, medical attention may be needed. Odd as this technique may seem, it's quite safe. If you happen to have active oral herpes, however, you should keep your mouth away from your child's face and try some other means to remove the foreign body from the eye.

FALLS

Falls with their accompanying scrapes, bumps, and bruises are an inevitable part of a child's first few years. In most cases, no harm is done. Here are some points to keep in mind, however, as your child learns to walk and climb.

• You can't always prevent the normal little falls of a child learning to become independently mobile, nor should you exhaust yourself trying. However, you can and *must* eliminate situations in which a fall could cause serious injury. Windows must be secure and those above the first floor should have safety guards. Stairs should have gates. No child should be unsupervised long enough to climb to a height from which a fall could be serious. When a child reaches the climbing and falling out of the crib stage, make alternative sleeping arrangements such as a mattress on the floor.

• If your child has fallen, be alert for signs of head injury. Loss of consciousness, onset of vomiting, bleeding from the ears, nose, or mouth, lack of eye response or one pupil noticeably larger than the other are symptoms of a possible problem after a fall. If your child has fallen, and one or more of these conditions follows, call the doctor right away.

• Unusual loss of appetite or excessive sleepiness after a fall may also signal a problem. Be alert to any difficulty or discomfort your child has moving one or more limbs after a fall. When in doubt, consult a doctor.

FAMILY BEDS

Are family beds a good idea, a bad idea, or neither? The family bed—parents and young children sleeping together—is a child rearing issue which, at present, is quite controversial. At one extreme are proponents of co-family sleeping who advocate permitting and encouraging children to sleep in the family bed for as many months or years as each child wishes to do so. At the other extreme are certain child-rearing "experts" who advise letting children cry it out each night until they finally realize that separation at bedtime is inevitable. For the toddler who can climb from the crib and invite him- or herself to the family bed, one well-known physician suggests using a badminton net to cover the top of the crib at night to keep the child in his or her place. Most families would choose a course somewhere in between those positions.

Family bed enthusiasts, led by Tine Thevenin, author of *The Family Bed,* claim that their children are happier, more secure, and ultimately less dependent than children who are forced to sleep alone. Others such as psychologist John Rosemond, author of *Parent Power: A Common Sense Approach to Raising Your Children in the Eighties,* strongly disagree and cite excessive dependence, anxiety, and social immaturity of the children along with widespread parental dissatisfaction about the family bed arrangements.

Although sleeping arrangements are social behaviors strongly influenced by the culture in which we live, they are also a very private matter and must suit the personal preferences of the people involved. What other people think and do should not be terribly important to you as long as your sleeping arrangements work for *your* family. Nevertheless, you can learn from others' mistakes. Here are some points to ponder before you and your children decide that sharing the same bed is a solution to sleepy-time problems.

• The family bed isn't something that can be tried out casually to see if you like it. Although many nursing mothers find that a newborn's night feedings are most comfortably accomplished in the parents' bed, don't make a practice of taking your mobile baby or toddler into your bed unless you are prepared to continue this for a long time—months, or perhaps even years. Once started, the family bed is a difficult practice to stop until the child is willing.

• Sleeping in one's own bed involves separation which for a young child (and parents too) includes some anxiety. Learning how to cope with this is an important aspect of growing up. A secure, supportive, and warm family environment can help a child take these steps toward independence. Parents can give a child support, warmth, and security in many other ways.

• Many couples feel that the quality of their own relationship depends in part on private time together. Making bedtime and the night that follows a family event diminishes the time available for parents to be alone together. If tensions result, it does the children no good.

• Taking a screaming child into your bed every night because the child refuses to settle down in his or her own bed will probably achieve the immediate goal of peace and quiet so everyone can get some sleep. However, it may also teach the child that you can be manipulated and controlled by his or her screaming. There are other techniques to make your child feel secure and content enough to go to sleep.

If you truly feel that sharing the family bed with your child would be a positive step toward enhancing your family life and meeting everyone's needs, then you should feel free to take that step if you wish. Hopefully it will work well for you. If, however, you're considering the family bed in desperation because bedtime is battletime and nothing else seems to work, we strongly suggest that you reconsider and attempt another approach. For suggestions on how to manage bedtime problems in a sensitive, caring way without inviting your child into bed with you, see Bedtime (Rituals), page 26 and Sleep Problems, page 118.

FAMILY PLANNING

The number of children you decide to have, and how you space them, shouldn't be anyone else's business, although many people—friends, relatives, and even casual acquaintances—often seem willing to offer opinions on such matters.

There are advantages and disadvantages to being an only child, or to being one of several siblings—to being close together in age, or to being several years apart. The only guideline we would offer on this very personal matter is that each child you choose to have should be wanted for his or her own sake, rather than as a companion for another child, as glue for the parents' relationship, or to please or impress other relatives or friends.

There is no one right way to plan a family, so you should try to do what makes the most sense to you in your particular circumstances.

FEARS

Many young children have fears which to an adult might seem somewhat silly. Such fears are, however, very significant to the child involved, and efforts to make light of them generally serve no purpose other than to convince the child that he or she can't count on the adults close by for support. Among the common fears of the toddler age are separation (see Separation Anxiety, page 111), baths (see Baths, page 21), dogs, insects, loud noises, shadows, and the dark. Make an effort not to communicate any fears you might have to your child. Some childhood fears are learned from adult caretakers, and there's no need to let this happen.

To help you deal with your child's specific fears in a sensitive way, first try putting yourself in his or her place. Imagine what it must be like to be a person of such small size in an enormous world. Try to remember back to your own childhood if you can, and recall things that you found frightening. Are there things which still scare you even though you know they'll probably cause no harm? For example, think about how you might react at this moment if a mouse (substitute snake, or whatever it is you fearfully dislike) were to leap onto the page as you were reading. Why would it be any more silly for a toddler to recoil and dissolve into tears at the sight of the neighbor's dog which, to a tiny person, could easily appear to be a ferocious monster?

Before your child is able to use language well enough to tell you what he or she is afraid of, you'll have to look for other clues. Sudden tears and efforts to move away from something are, of course, the obvious clues. Extra clinginess to you is another indication that something is causing fear.

How should you cope with a fearful child? Be reassuring and supportive, but be careful to support the child and not the fear. For example, say "I know that the big dog frightens you. It must

be scary to be so small next to an animal that big. But don't worry, I'm here to hold your hand and the dog won't hurt you." This is far better than "What an awful horrible dog to frighten my little girl (boy). I'll have to chase the monster away before it hurts you." Be supportive and protective, but don't add validity to the fear.

Even if the feared thing is likely to cause no harm, it's unwise to force this thing on your child in an effort to prove to the child that the fear is unfounded. Don't, for example, drag the child who's afraid of dogs past every canine in the neighborhood for a chat and a pat. Don't toss the water-fearful toddler into the pool and hope for a cure. Such an approach is unlikely to foster bravery, and it might help turn an ordinary fear into a phobia. A phobia is a fear carried to such an intense degree that it interferes with a person's ability to function. A child with a fear of dogs won't want to go near a dog when one is around, but won't spend the rest of the time thinking about what might happen in case a dog should appear. In contrast, a child with a phobia about dogs won't go near a dog, and also might panic at the bark of a dog, the mention of the word dog, a picture of a dog, the sight of anything that resembles the shape of a dog, the supermarket where there frequently is a terrier tied outside, the lawn where two dogs were playing last week, and perhaps even the thought of going outside because there might be dogs somewhere. If your child has a fear that has escalated into a phobia, you may need professional help in dealing with it.

If your efforts to handle the normal toddler fears in a kind and reassuring way don't quite do the job or if a phobia is upsetting your child, ask your child's pediatrician for advice. Above all, don't make matters worse by resorting to ridicule, shame, or punishment to make the child stop being afraid of something. These tactics won't work, and no matter how unreasonable the child's fears may seem to you, to the child they're real and you are his or her protector.

FEEDING (How and When)

Breast-fed and bottle-fed babies are usually fed on demand. For detailed information on feeding a newborn, see pages 13-34 of *Welcome Baby: A Guide to the First Six Weeks,* by Anne Marie Mueser and George Verrilli, (St. Martin's Press, New York: 1982).

Solid Foods (Introduction)

If you haven't yet introduced your baby to solid foods, when to do so is a decision you can make with the guidance of your child's pediatrician. In most cases, a child should be at least four months and probably closer to six months old before starting solid foods. Ignore the advice of the neighbor who insists that all her children slept through the night from the third week on because she weighed them down with cereal. Keep in mind that a baby's digestive system is too immature during the first few months to digest fully the nutrients in solid foods. There's no point in rushing.

When it is time to begin feeding your child solid foods, here are some suggestions:

• A single grain cereal is often the first food offered. Many parents find, however, that a smooth fruit such as commercially prepared baby applesauce is easier for the child to swallow at first, and they introduce the fruit a week or so before the first cereal bite. Either way is fine.

• Introduce no more than one new food in a week. If that item agrees with your child, then add another. For example, follow a week of mashed banana or strained applesauce with a week of the fruit mixed with barley or rice cereal.

How to Feed

A spoon with a tiny bowl is best for the first feedings. Don't force. Remember that taking nourishment from a spoon is an entirely new experience for a child who normally eats by sucking. Holding the spoon at the edge of the mouth and letting the child suck a bit of the food in may get you started. Expect that much of what goes in at first will come out without being swallowed. Don't lose patience or your sense of humor as you rescue the meal from the child's chin a spoonful at a time and try again.

During the early days of solid foods, your child will still be getting most of his or her nourishment from milk. If your child is very hungry at a particular meal, give some milk first—a few minutes on one breast or part of a bottle. A frantically hungry child is a poor candidate for learning how to take food from a spoon. After a bit of milk, try some spoon feeding before completing the rest of the meal with milk. If you give all the milk before offering the spoon, the child will be too comfortable to bother. So, the solid food portion of the meal should be in the middle.

When you are spoon feeding your child and he or she grabs the spoon, it's time to have a two spoon meal—one for you and one for him or her. This way you'll get some of the meal into the mouth as the child is learning to manipulate the spoon.

Some time during the second half of the first year (after you've introduced lumps into the strained foods), your child will be ready to start finger foods. A long thin piece of toast, a lump of cooked carrot or boiled potato, a string bean or a slice of beet are possible choices. The first experiences with finger foods will probably be more like play than like eating, but most children soon get the idea. Encourage your child to self-feed these items as much as possible.

Let your child develop his or her own style of self-feeding. It's too soon to deal with table manners in any way other than for *you* to use a fork instead of your fist when you eat your own dinner. Don't be upset if your child makes unusual (to you) combinations as part of the eating fun. Who says peas don't belong in the custard or minced meat in the orange juice?

There really isn't any one right way to feed a child. Do what makes sense and encourage your child to take as active and independent a role in the feeding as possible.

Feeding Schedule

When you introduce solid foods to your child, on what sort of a schedule should you feed? Chances are, by the time you begin solid foods, your child is (more or less) sleeping through the night. As you increase the solids and decrease the milk, you'll probably work toward three meals with snacks in between. Few toddlers can happily last from one major meal to the next, and a snack should be offered. However, avoid letting the child get into the habit of snacking nonstop. A midmorning and a midafternoon mini-meal will be sufficient.

FEEDING PROBLEMS

Many of the eating problems of early childhood are aided and abetted by well intentioned caregivers who themselves were brought up as members of the "clean plate club," or were encouraged to "eat a little more for the poor starving children of East Somewhere." Keep in mind that young children are natural survivors and, if appropriate food is made available to them, they usually take what they need. The child who becomes a fussy or picky eater is often one whose parents have made a big deal about eating neatly or cleaning the plate. Parental efforts to force food, when added to a toddler's natural contrariness, result in a volatile mixture which does neither the child nor the parents any good. Don't let your efforts to feed your child well end up creating more problems than they solve. Here are some suggestions.

• Remember that it's impossible for a baby or toddler to be neat, and don't let the inevitable mess create tensions at mealtime.

• As soon as possible, let your child actively participate in self-feeding. Most children will make these efforts by the first birthday, although some will take a bit longer. The time to give your child a chance to be independent is when he or she first shows an interest. If you continue to push the spoon long after he or she is able to take on this task, you may find that your child has become used to dependence on you at mealtime and will be reluctant to give it up.

• Provide a balanced diet (see Nutrition, page 98), over a period of time such as a week or two. Don't worry about balancing each meal, because it's next to impossible to do so without creating problems.

• Don't panic if your toddler goes through stages of seeming to eat less than usual, very little, or even nothing at all for a meal or two. This is normal. Between growth spurts, many children cut down on food consumption. Unless there is some other reason to suspect illness or a problem, it's fine to let your child's appetite determine how much he or she will eat, and you shouldn't be concerned even if *you* think the quantity is not sufficient.

• At any meal, when your child is no longer hungry, separate the child from the rest of the food and consider the mealtime finished. Do this without comment even if you wish the child had eaten more. Skip the "Eat another bite for Daddy" and "Now one more for Aunt Maggie" routine. Such tactics only add unnecessary emotional baggage to the act of eating. Remember that the child's purpose for eating should involve his or her own nourishment. Don't confuse the issue for either of you.

• Permit your child to have personal preferences in food and recognize that these preferences, especially during the toddler years, are likely to change many times. If you go out of your way to force a food that your toddler temporarily dislikes, the child may continue to dislike that food out of sheer stubbornness. If you avoid making a moral issue out of food choices, you stand a better chance of having your toddler eat what's best for him or her in the long run.

• Respecting your child's preferences does not mean, however, that you should get into the habit of running a restaurant which caters to your child's every culinary whim. Offer variety, and chances are your child will do just fine. Try to serve foods your child will like, but don't be surprised if toddler tastes change often in unpredictable ways. If your child rejects everything offered, try again at the next meal, but don't prepare three different lunches hoping to get to one he or she likes. It won't be long before the child's hunger and survival instincts begin to work in favor of whatever it is you are serving. There's no need to serve pureed pizza seven nights a week even if your child demands it. Use common sense and be reassured that your child will not deliberately starve.

FEVER

There's only one way to tell for sure if your child has a fever, and that's to use a thermometer to take his or her temperature. Feeling the child's forehead with your hand is not an accurate source of information. Digital forehead strips are not accurate either. Use a thermometer.

If you think your child is sick, and you decide to call the doctor, take the child's temperature before your call. The doctor will ask you what the temperature is, and you might as well have the information ready. (The exception to this is, of course, if you are dealing with an emergency situation, in which case make the call without wasting any time.)

A normal rectal temperature for a child is 99.6 degrees F. (37.6 degrees C.). If you use the axillary (armpit) method, a normal temperature is 97.6 degrees F. (36.7 degrees C.) Taking the temperature of a baby or small child by mouth is not recommended. (See Temperature (Taking Child's), page 132.)

Call the doctor if your child's rectal temperature is above 100.6 F. and other symptoms of illness are present.

It's important to remember that fever is a symptom, and not the disease itself. Fever generally indicates that the body is fighting an infection (bacterial or viral) of some kind. It's not usually necessary to take extraordinary measures to combat the fever directly unless it's over 102° F. Try to keep the child comfortable in a room that's not overheated. The child should be dressed in lightweight fabrics and covered with a lightweight blanket or perhaps only a sheet.

For fever of 103° or higher, or if your doctor directs you to try to bring the fever down, undress the child and sponge off the skin's surface with a washcloth saturated with lukewarm (not cold) water. (If your child starts to shiver, that

72

means the water is too cold.) As the water evaporates off the skin's surface the child should become cooler.

Don't administer medication without consulting the doctor. Avoid aspirin for an infant under a year old or for any child with a virus (or suspected virus) infection such as a cold or influenza. If your doctor recommends that you give the child acetaminophen ("fever drops" such as liquid Tylenol), be sure to follow the recommended dosage for your child's age exactly. Twice the dose is not twice as good, and an overdose can cause serious harm.

FIRE

Fires in the home are a major cause of accidental death and serious injury in young children. Here are some tips on preventing fires and protecting your family if a fire should break out.

• Check out your home carefully and eliminate any obvious fire hazards—for example, faulty wiring, frayed appliance cords, or stored flammable materials.

• Keep your child well apart from matches, space heaters, fireplaces, stoves, etc.

• Install a smoke alarm on each level of your house, or at least one in the bedroom area. (See Smoke Detectors, page 119.)

• A smoke alarm can wake you, but it can't lead you outside. Plan in advance what escape route you would take to get yourself and your child out of the house in the event of a fire. Plan an alternate route to use if the fire should block your intended exit path. For floors above ground level, a fire exit ladder is something a homeowner should keep handy. Have a family fire drill and rehearse getting out.

• Identify your child's bedroom window with a symbol to let firefighters know at a glance where their assistance in rescue might be needed. Highly visible decals are available for this purpose from many local fire departments. Ask.

Clothes on Fire

If a child's clothes catch on fire, act quickly to put it out. Save the lecture on not playing with matches for later. Use a coat or a rug to smother the flames. Or, if there's nothing handy to smother the flames you can do so with your own body. Put the child down on the ground with the flames on the side facing up. Cover the child quickly and completely with your body, which will deprive the fire of oxygen and extinguish it without causing you injury. Treat the burns as necessary. (See Burns and Scalds, page 35.)

FLUORIDE

It is generally agreed that fluoride is an effective aid in preventing tooth decay. If the water in your area is fluoridated, you won't have to give this matter any further thought. If your water supply contains less than 0.3 parts per million of fluoride, your child's doctor may prescribe a fluoride supplement. These supplements are available by prescription in liquid form, in combination with liquid vitamins, or as chewable tablets. If your water supply contains more than one part per million of fluoride, you should not give your child a fluoride supplement. Too much can be toxic or can cause discoloration of the tooth enamel. If you are uncertain of the amount of fluoride in the water you use, consult the local health department or your pediatrician.

If a fluoride supplement is necessary where you live, consult your child's doctor who will advise you about which supplement to use and when to begin it. Some doctors endorse use of a fluoride supplement within the first few weeks. Others prefer to wait until a child is several months old before beginning treatment.

GENITALS (Care of)

The genitals of your baby or toddler require no special care other than the bathing you give the entire diaper area to keep it clean and free from irritation. Don't attempt to force back the foreskin of an uncircumcised boy in an effort to clean under it. Don't push apart a girl's labia for washing. A good rule for care of your child's genitals is to leave alone what you can't see. Regular bathing is all that's necessary.

GIFTED CHILDREN

In today's high pressure society, many parents wonder and worry very early about the abilities and talents of their children. Is the child gifted? What does it mean to be "gifted," anyway? What special measures should be taken to prepare a child for the best nursery school, college or graduate school? Should you really be worrying about all this when your child isn't two years old yet?

Is your child gifted? Every child is gifted in his or her own way. Whether those gifts ultimately add up to a high score on an IQ test, early admission to a good college or stardom as a concert musician is far less important at this point than the process of learning to learn. What we suggest is that you enjoy learning with your child. Provide suitable stimulation and learning experiences and nurture without undue pressure your child's many different abilities as they emerge and develop. (See pages 88-92 for specific activities to help you do this.) Just as children differ greatly in appearance, they differ in the combination of strengths and weaknesses in their various abilities and talents. If you concentrate on the uniqueness of your child and encourage his or her curiosity, creativity, and excitement about life and learning, you'll be helping to maximize the special gifts your child has.

GROWTH

At routine well-child visits to your child's pediatrician or healthcare clinic, your child's height and weight will be measured and recorded. If you wish to keep track of your child's rate of growth, ask your pediatrician for a chart on which you can record the measurements. Your child's doctor will keep a chart on file, but may be willing to provide a duplicate for you to record your child's growth between visits.

For a child too young to stand tall and still, measure the length while the child is lying down. Two adults are needed to do this accurately. For a child who can and will stand, a flat stick (such as a ruler) can be held on top of the child's head at right angles to the wall. Mark the wall where the stick touches, and then measure the distance from the mark to the floor. (The child should be barefoot.) For recording the child's weight, use the same scale each time.

HANDEDNESS

Although most babies begin using both hands rather equally, preference for one or the other may develop early. Some children seem to favor one hand and then switch to the other, perhaps even changing back again before establishing dominance.

How should you deal with handedness? Here are some hints.

• If your child favors the right hand, be thankful for it. Many of the world's structures are arranged for the convenience of right-handed people.

• If your child seems strongly to favor the left hand, let it be. More harm will come from forceful efforts to make him or her change. (See Left-Handed Children, page 92.) Be supportive and avoid criticism.

• For a child who isn't yet sure about his or her preference, you may be able to influence the choice although chances are what will be, will be. Offer food, the spoon, toys, or other objects to the right hand if you wish. However, if the child develops preference for the left despite your efforts, don't fight it.

HANDICAPPED CHILDREN

If any aspect of your child's development causes you concern, don't hesitate to ask your child's physician about it. If you suspect a developmental handicap — mental or physical — pretending there's nothing wrong won't make the problem go away. Ask for a full evaluation of your child if you have reason to think there's a problem. If your child is handicapped in some way, early intervention is important.

A child with a specific handicap should be supported or encouraged to develop normally in whatever areas that development is possible. Make every effort to limit the effects of the handicap to the function that is impaired, and help the child to develop as fully as possible in other ways. You should actively seek whatever assistance is available from state agencies and support groups of parents with a similarly handicapped child. Your physician may be able to advise you of specific facilities in your area.

Here are some addresses from which further information about specific handicaps can be obtained.

Action for Brain Handicapped Children
300 Wilder Building
St. Paul, MN 55102
(Information for parents and professionals.)

Alexander Graham Bell Association for the
    Deaf, Inc.
International Parents' Organization
1537 35 Street NW
Washington, DC 20016
(Information for parents of children with
    hearing problems.)

Allergy Foundation of America
801 Second Avenue
New York, NY 10017
(Information and work with healthcare
    providers.)

American Academy of Child Psychiatry
1800 R Street NW, Suite 904
Washington, DC 20009
(Information on services available.)

American Academy of Pediatrics
1801 Hinman Avenue
Evanston, IL 60204
(Information on common childhood
    problems.)

American Cleft Palate Education Foundation
331 Salk Hall
University of Pittsburgh
Pittsburgh, PA 15261
(Information and referral services.)

American Council for the Blind
818 18 Street NW, Suite 700
Washington, DC 20006
(Clearinghouse for information and services.)

American Foundation for the Blind
15 West 16 Street
New York, NY 10011
(Clearinghouse for information and available
    services.)

American Speech & Hearing Association
10801 Rockville Pike
Rockville, MD 20852
(Information and referrals for children with
    speech or hearing problems.)

Association for Children with Learning
    Disabilities
4156 Library Road
Pittsburgh, PA 15234
(Information and referrals.)

Council for Exceptional Children
1920 Association Drive
Reston, VA 22090
(Information for parents of handicapped or
    gifted children.)

Epilepsy Foundation of America
1828 L Street NW, Suite 406
Washington, DC 20036
(Referrals to local agencies.)

Family Service Association of America
44 East 23 Street
New York, NY 10010
(Referrals to local agencies.)

Foundation for Child Development
345 East 46th Street
New York, NY 10017
(Information and referrals.)

National Association for Hearing and Speech
  Action
814 Thayer Avenue
Silver Spring, MD 20910
(Information and referrals.)

National Hemophilia Foundation, Inc
25 West 39th Street
New York, NY 10018
(Information and referrals.)

National Association for Mental Health
1800 North Kent Street
Rosslyn Station
Arlington, VA 22209
(Information.)

National Association for Retarded Citizens
2709 Avenue E East
Arlington, TX 76001
(Clearinghouse for information and services.)

National Asthma Center
875 Avenue of the Americas
New York, NY 10001
(Information and referral for treatment.)

National Easter Seal Society for Crippled
  Children and Adults
2303 West Ogden Avenue
Chicago, IL 60612
(Information and services for the
  handicapped.)

National Foundation—March of Dimes
Box 2000
White Plains, NY 10602
(Information, research, and services relating
  to birth defects and crippling conditions.)

National Society for Autistic Children
621 Central Avenue
Albany, NY 12206
(Information and referrals.)

Sickle Cell Disease Foundation
209 West 125 Street
New York, NY 10027
(Information and referrals.)

Society for the Facially Disfigured
550 First Avenue
New York, NY 10016
(Information and referrals.)

Spina Bifida Association of America
P.O. Box 266
Newcastle, DE
(Information and referrals.)

United Cerebral Palsy Foundation
66 East 34 Street
New York, NY 10010
(Information and referrals.)

United States Public Health Service
National Institutes of Health
Public Information Officer
Bethesda, MD 20014
(Information about birth defects.)

HEAD BANGING (Severe)

Some babies or toddlers develop a habit of head banging, in which the head is hit rhythmically against something hard. For the child so inclined, this habit often accompanies bedtime, when the crib sides are the object being hit. Some children rock so fiercely on their hands and knees, striking the head with each rock, that the crib actually moves across the room. If not in the crib, some children bang on walls or pieces of furniture.

If your child is a head banger, don't ignore this behavior. Of course, the first line of defense is to pad the crib so the child doesn't get hurt. But don't stop there. Try to figure out why your child has resorted to such an extreme form of comfort seeking. Although some experts would place head banging in the same category as thumb sucking or cuddling a "lovey," we feel that a severe case of head banging (which causes pain) is cause for concern. It may indicate that the child is angry, tense, or insecure for some reason. While some such feelings may be a normal part of growing up, it's likely that a child whose response is self-inflicted pain is trying to tell you something. It's best not to ignore the message. If extra doses of kind, positive attention throughout the day, as well as careful attention to bedtime rituals bring no improvement, you may want to seek professional guidance. (See Comfort Habits, page 45.)

HEARING (Problems)

Even before birth, a healthy baby is able to hear. Newborns show signs of responding to sounds right from the start. A loud noise will usually startle a baby. Most newborns are soothed by the parent's voice and will turn the head seeking the source of the sound (even though the turn might be in the wrong direction at first).

As your child grows, you'll want to be alert to any possible signs of hearing loss and have your child's hearing professionally tested if you suspect any problem. Here are some observations you can make informally:

6–8 months	Does your baby turn toward the source of familiar sounds? If it appears that he or she does not, try it out a few times with a familiar sound located three or four feet away. If the baby does not turn, mention this to your pediatrician and request a hearing evaluation.
1 year	Does your baby seem to be trying to talk (even if it doesn't sound much like real talking)? If not, have the hearing checked. Babies learn to talk by imitating, and they have nothing to imitate if they can't hear.
18 months	Can your child use simple words? Can he or she follow a simple spoken direction? If not, hearing loss may be part of the problem. Have it checked.
2 years	If you tell your child to do something (without using gestures or other visual clues) can he or she follow the direction you give? (Don't confuse the contrary child who *won't* because you said so with the child who *can't* because he or she couldn't hear.) Can your child repeat a three-word sentence or simple phrase? Can your child recognize an object by its sound? If these things seem to be a problem for your two-year-old, have the hearing checked.

If your child does have a hearing problem, the earlier treatment or corrective intervention is started, the better. Sometimes the effects of hearing loss are not recognized for what they are and a child is incorrectly labeled retarded, emotionally disturbed, or learning disabled. A thorough hearing evaluation by an appropriate professional should be done if you have any suspicion of a hearing problem in your child. (See also Ears, page 63.)

HEAT RASH (Prickly Heat)

In hot weather, many children get a rash called prickly heat—very tiny pink pimples and blotches and perhaps some blisters. Prickly heat usually begins around the neck and shoulders. In severe cases it may spread to the rest of the body. You'll probably worry about it more than it will trouble your child, but you should take care of it promptly even if he or she doesn't appear to be bothered.

The best treatment is also the key to prevention. Keep your child dressed appropriately for the weather. Remove clothes if the weather is very hot. A light dusting with baby powder or cornstarch might help. Take care that the child doesn't breathe in any of the powder. Sprinkle it on your hands, and then apply it gently to the child's skin. Don't shake it directly on the child.

Heat rash is not only a summer problem. It is also common in winter, when babies and toddlers tend to be overdressed in heated houses, cars, or stores.

HERNIAS

An umbilical hernia is the most common type of hernia. It is a small swelling near the navel of a baby, and its cause is weakness of the muscles in that area. The bulge may increase somewhat when the baby cries. Although tight strapping used to be the prescribed treatment for an umbilical hernia, it is now believed that the area will strengthen best on its own. Most cases of umbilical hernia put themselves right within a year or two without any treatment at all. In very rare cases, surgery may be indicated.

An inguinal hernia, which occurs most often in boys, is an opening in the abdonominal wall muscles allowing a portion of the intestine to squeeze into the groin area. A "strangulated" inguinal hernia is one in which the intestine has become stuck in the passage, causing severe pain and requiring prompt emergency treatment.

If you think your baby might have a hernia, consult your doctor. Chances are, if you have taken your child for regular well-baby checkups, any signs of a hernia will have been discovered.

HIGH CHAIRS AND FEEDING TABLES

When your baby is old enough to sit up unassisted for a meal, then you'll have to decide how, where, and on what you want him or her to sit. Check out the pros and cons of high chairs vs. feeding tables before you make a decision and buy one.

High Chairs

If you are thinking about a high chair for your child, keep these points in mind.

• The chair should be sturdy with a wide base so an active baby or toddler won't be able to tip it over. Shake a chair before you buy it. See how stable it is.

• A removable tray is easier to clean than one which is permanently attached to the chair. A badly designed removable tray can pinch fingers and dislodge when it shouldn't. Check the particular model you're considering very carefully.

• The chair needs a crotch strap to keep your child from making a hasty exit beneath the tray.

• A high chair with tray removed or back out of the way can be used to let an older toddler sit at the family table and still reach his or her dinner. This is a plus.

• A child should not be left unsupervised in a high chair. It's a long way to the floor.

Feeding Tables

Here are some things to think about before you decide to buy a feeding table for your child.

• Feeding tables are generally safer than high chairs. They're less likely to tip over and a climbing toddler hasn't as far to fall.

• The large table surface means less food and drink on the floor when the meal is done. (It's on the table top instead.)

• A feeding table takes considerably more space than a high chair, and the child is at a level lower than much of the interesting adult activity nearby.

• You can't use a feeding table at the family dinner table. If there's room, however, you could place it nearby. This does set the child apart.

• Although theoretically a feeding table's surface can be used for activities other than putting food in front of your toddler, many parents find that the device is not nearly as practical as they had hoped. Chances are your toddler won't want to sit that confined for any significant period of time no matter what enticing objects you place on the table.

Homemade Substitutes

A high chair or feeding table—take your pick—is really a must for those many months between the time your child has stopped feeding quietly in your arms and the wonderful day when he or she can take full part in family mealtime without causing great disruption. There will, however, be times and places where you won't have access to the furniture you need. What should you do when you are visiting or if another family's toddler has just been seated in the restaurant's only high chair? What if you are given a booster seat without a strap?

If you frequently take your toddler with you for meals outside the home, you might find it handy to purchase a plastic booster seat. This lightweight device fits in a large shopping bag, and can be placed on a regular chair to bring your toddler closer to table level. It does not work well, however, for a child who is extremely active because it can be wiggled off the chair. In a restaurant (or anywhere), a safety strap can be improvised out of large cloth napkins securely tied together. A child should never be tied into a chair, however, if you're not right there to make sure nothing goes wrong. If a booster seat is unavailable, a firm pillow, a folded coat, or a thick telephone book can serve as a booster Chances are if you look around you'll find something that will work for a little while at least.

HOSPITALIZATION

If your child has to go to a hospital for any reason, and you have time to prepare for it, there are a number of steps you can take to make what is inevitably a traumatic situation a little easier. Here are some suggestions.

• If the hospital permits a parent to room in with the child, by all means do so. If not, make sure you can spend significant portions of the child's waking hours with him or her.

• Find out as much as possible about the facilities and procedures that are planned for your child to enable you to prepare him or her for what's in store.

• Be as honest with your child about what's going to happen as you can without being unnecessarily alarming. Don't promise painless procedures if that promise would be a lie. Say instead that the doctor can give something to help if it hurts. Don't promise daily pizza, ice cream, or sweets, if intravenous feeding or bland hospital food is all that's in the offing.

• Try to prepare the child for any procedure which may be especially stressful —for example, X-rays, injections, intravenous drips.

• Discuss your child's case completely with the physicians handling it so that you feel fully informed and as comfortable as possible about the procedures. Don't be afraid to ask questions and demand answers.

Emergency Treatment

If your child is hospitalized because of an emergency—sudden illness or accident—there will be no time for elaborate preparations. Under such circumstances, it's even more important for you to remain with your child so that feelings of abandonment aren't added to the other traumas. Remember that it's your child and you have a right to be with him or her and to be kept informed of what's going on. Insist on staying around, and don't be intimidated by hospital personnel who would rather have you go home and call them in the morning.

a hospital stay, many children regress a bit in level of behavior. Don't be
ed if this happens. When your child returns home he or she may be more
Jent and seem to cling to you more. Some children demand to go back
to a bottle even though previously weaned. A hospital stay can undo toilet
training, so be patient and buy disposable diapers for nighttime for a little while
if necessary. Your child may even blame you for his or her predicament, and act
angry for a while. Extra support and solace are in order.

> To help prepare a preschool child for a hospital
> stay, you might use the book *Curious George Goes
> to the Hospital,* by Margret and H.A. Rey, in
> collaboration with the Children's Hospital Medical
> Center, Boston (Houghton Mifflin Co., Boston:
> 1966). This humorously illustrated book, available in
> paperback, features the popular little monkey
> whose curiosity frequently gets him into trouble.

HYPERACTIVITY

What is hyperactivity? There are some children who, for specific medical
reasons, have a short attention span, extreme distractability, and very high
activity level. Such children, if diagnosed as hyperactive by a physician
(preferably a pediatric neurologist), may benefit from treatment including
dietary changes and/or medication. Unfortunately, these days, many people
apply the label hyperactive to numerous energetic, healthy, and normally active
youngsters. Many of the behaviors characteristic of a hyperactive child
are typical also of all or most normal toddlers. A two-year-old with more
energy than his or her caregivers is admittedly a handful, but not necessarily
(and probably not) hyperactive. A correct medical diagnosis of hyperactivity
would be very difficult to make for any toddler because the high activity level is
normal for the age. Attaching the label "hyperactive" to a child does nothing
positive for the child, but gives a handy excuse to adults who can't cope.

What should you do if your toddler is busily driving you up the wall with
energy you can't match? Some children are tougher to live with than others, and
no toddler is easy all of the time. Here are some suggestions for coping with an
extremely active child, whether or not a medical diagnosis of hyperactivity
would be warranted.

• Consciously and deliberately build more structure into the child's day.
Predictable and careful attention to routines and rituals may help. Set
guidelines which are easily understood by the child. (For example, spread a
plastic tablecloth on the floor and tell the child that the toys can be dumped
out there. This won't entirely keep blocks from turning up underfoot or in odd
corners, but it will start to introduce the notion of limits.)

• Childproofing your house, while necessary for all young children, is especially important for a child whose activity level is high. You may choose to remove not only those objects which could cause harm, but also some of those which could cause instant chaos as well. For example, you might find it easier to move the entire contents of your silverware drawer (not simply the sharp knives) and give your child two or three wooden spoons to play with instead of picking up the service for eight five times a morning.

• Try to be consistent. If it's not acceptable for your child to remove all the books from the bookcase today, then it shouldn't be O.K. to do it next weekend when you're in a better mood. Make reasonable decisions about what you will and won't tolerate, and try to stick to what you've decided. (You needn't be rigid, and if you've made a silly decision of course you should change it, but you should avoid confusing the child with a lot of constantly shifting limits.)

• Provide suitable stimulation for your child. Many children with high activity level are very bright and also very bored. The availability of interesting activities requiring active involvement may help channel a child's energies into constructive and appropriate experiences. (See pages 88-92.)

• Don't fall into the trap of depending on television to help you keep your active child occupied and under control even though he or she may seem willing to sit in front of the tube for more than a few minutes at a stretch. The rapidly changing images on the screen are probably not building attention span as you might hope, but are bombarding the child with stimulation while providing no structure for the child to respond. Television's mesmerizing effect on your child may on occasion give you some respite from your child's activity level, but it won't solve your long term problem and may even make it worse.

• Because some research has suggested a possible link between hyperactivity in some children and consumption of foods containing artificial colors or flavors, avoiding foods with artificial colors and flavors is worth a try. Excess sugar in the diet has also been blamed for hyperactivity, and reduction of your child's sugar consumption may be useful. (Whether or not your child shows a tendency toward hyperactivity, eliminating artificial colors and flavors and excessive sweets from the diet is a step toward better nutrition.)

• Caffeine is an ingredient which should be avoided in any child's diet, and especially in the diet of a child with hyperactive tendencies. A child with high energy and activity level does not need caffeine, which is a stimulant. Coffee, tea, and cola drinks should not be a part of a toddler's routine.

IMMUNIZATIONS

A number of childhood diseases which were common two or three generations ago are now quite rare because of widespread immunization programs. Immunizations are an important part of a comprehensive health care program for your child. Don't let the infrequency of certain diseases lull you into a false sense of security and tempt you to skip your child's "shots." A complete series of immunizations is required for school entry in many communities. And, if any significant number of parents decided to forego the immunizations for their own children, it probably wouldn't be long before some of these diseases were reestablished as a serious problem.

Recommended Schedule of Immunizations

Try to follow the recommended schedule of immunizations. If you plan to travel out of the country, be sure to mention this to your physician in case additional immunizations or a change in the prescribed schedule might be indicated. Some childhood diseases which have been almost eliminated in the United States still occur in places where many children remain unvaccinated.

RECORD OF IMMUNIZATIONS

	RECOMMENDED AGE*	DATE GIVEN	REACTION
DTP (diphtheria, tetanus & pertussis)	2 months		
DTP	4 months		
DTP	6 months		
DTP	1½ yrs.		
DTP	4-6 yrs.		
ORAL POLIO VACCINE	2 months		
ORAL POLIO VACCINE	4 months		
ORAL POLIO VACCINE	6 months (optional)		
ORAL POLIO VACCINE	1½ yrs.		
ORAL POLIO VACCINE	4-6 yrs.		
MEASLES MUMPS RUBELLA (German measles) } usually given as MMR	15 months		
OTHERS, AS NEEDED			

TEST FOR TB, while not an immunization, is usually given at one year.

*Immunization schedule recommended by the American Academy of Pediatrics.

Reactions

Some children do show a reaction to certain immunizations, but the possibility of such a reaction is generally not a reason to avoid the immunization. The reaction is almost never as severe as the complications from the disease might have been. Feel free, however, to discuss any concerns you might have about this with your child's physician. Observe your child carefully after an immunization and call the doctor if your child seems to be reacting in an unusual way or if you are concerned about the reaction.

After the DTP immunization, there may be some soreness at the spot of the injection, and many children seem cranky or out of sorts for a day. If your child develops a fever or seems really sick after a DTP injection, call the doctor for advice. Some children react badly to the pertussis (whooping cough) component of the triple vaccine and the doctor may decide to modify the dose used in future boosters.

Many children experience some fever, discomfort, and a mild rash about a week after the measles immunization (usually given as MMR, in combination with vaccines for mumps and rubella). Your child's physician will tell you what to do if this occurs.

INDEPENDENCE

As your toddler strives for independence, you should try to encourage and support this independent behavior in whatever areas you can do so without compromising the child's safety. There will be many times when you'll be sorely tempted to take over and do the task yourself just to get it done, but you should try to resist this impulse whenever you can. For example, when your child insists on dressing himself or herself, a compliment is in order even if he or she gets the shirt backwards, the pants a little twisted, the sweater buttoned wrong, and socks that don't match—all in about five times as long as it would have taken you to dress the child beautifully. No one (but yourself) will care or even notice the shirt and the socks, and you can help straighten out the sweater without any notice. Remember that your child is learning, and tomorrow is another day and another chance to get it right. If you insist on doing everything for your child instead of encouraging independence when your child starts to try things on his or her own, you may find you're still a personal valet when your offspring reaches school age.

Eating is another area of behavior in which it's best to permit your child to become independent as soon as he or she shows signs of doing do. While it's nice for you to be the provider of nourishment, you don't personally have to dispense this nourishment a spoonful at a time once your child has figured out how to get food from the plate to the mouth without your help. Self-feeding by a toddler is messier to be sure, but it's an essential ingredient of becoming independent.

Although there will be many times in a day to encourage your child's independence, and you should take advantage of these times, never forget that a toddler's reach often exceeds his or her judgment. Don't permit your child to exercise independence in ways that could be dangerous—for example, climbing a tree, swimming in the pool, operating an appliance, walking the dog in traffic, or crossing a street. Use common sense as you permit your youngster to try his or her fledgling wings.

JUICE

When should you first offer juice to your baby? To provide needed vitamin C, some doctors suggest offering orange juice as early as three months. Others prefer that you delay juice until six months or later, when sensitivity to citrus fruits is less likely. A liquid vitamin supplement may be used instead. (See Vitamin Supplements, page 144.) Many babies enjoy apple juice fortified with vitamin C which is less likely to trigger an allergic reaction. It's best to follow your pediatrician's advice about what juices to offer your baby and when to begin.

As with any new food, start slowly to make sure that your child can handle it. Unless the doctor directs otherwise, start with a small quantity of juice (not more than a tablespoon) diluted with an equal amount of water. Add an additional teaspoonful of juice each day and then gradually decrease the water until your child is drinking two to three ounces of undiluted juice. This is enough for a child up to six months. More may leave too little room for other needed nutrients. A daily serving of four ounces is recommended for older babies and toddlers. Work up to it gradually, increasing the amount a little bit each day.

Here are some additional notes about juice for your child:

• Commercially prepared orange juice is fine or you may squeeze fresh oranges and strain the juice yourself. It really doesn't matter. If you use concentrate, boil the water if your water supply is questionable. If your water is safe, mix the baby's juice as you would your own, adding additional water to dilute if needed.

• Single serving bottles of baby juice are convenient but expensive. These are especially suitable for households in which the refrigerator might contain several open containers of juice, with some of doubtful freshness. With a single serving bottle, you can be sure that what you're giving the baby is fresh.

• Even unsweetened juices contain natural sugars which can add to the risk of tooth decay. Don't use juices in naptime or bedtime comfort bottles. By the age of six months or so, most children are able (with lots of help) and willing to sip their juice from a cup or a spoon.

• Don't use the syrup from canned fruit (even diluted with water) as a drink for your baby. This syrup is very high in sugar.

• Avoid commercially packaged fruit drinks, punches, or 'ades which are artificially colored and/or heavily sweetened, even if these products boast "Vitamin C added."

• Don't offer your child carbonated fruit-flavored beverages. These usually are heavily sweetened and contain artificial colorings. They are not nutritionally satisfactory substitutes for fruit juice, and there's no point in starting your child on the soda pop habit.

• The best commercial packages of orange juice or other acid foods are bottles or cardboard containers. Avoid cans, because the metal (especially the lead solder that seals the can) can leach into the contents. Never store chilled juice in an open can. This practice has been known to result in the lead-poisoning of young children.

JUNK FOODS

Junk foods are those which contain too many calories for the nutrients they provide, and many junk foods contain additives such as artificial flavorings and artificial colors. Unfortunately, many junk foods are packaged and advertised to be especially attractive to young children, and there may be times when you feel you are fighting a losing battle to confine your child's foods to those which are nutritionally sound.

Try not to get your child started on the junk food habit. Don't stock your cupboards with junk foods. Don't give in to a toddler's demands to purchase junk food even if it might save a tantrum in the supermarket aisle. Once you begin the practice of buying food items according to your child's whims, you may find it difficult to stop doing so. Encourage nutritious snacks such as fruits and raw vegetables. Juice and homemade milkshakes are preferable to sodas and the sugar laden shakes from fast food outlets.

An occasional meal in a fast food place, or a sweet snack from time to time, is not going to be the nutritional downfall of your child. Use common sense as you plan your child's meals, but don't fall into the trap of pushing nutritious items so hard that you give junk foods the added enticement of being forbidden. Practice what you preach. Your child is unlikely to be content with raw carrots while you sit there consuming Mallomars by the box.

KIDNAPPING

Each year, a frighteningly large number of young children—100,000 or more —disappear. Many of these are snatched by estranged spouses in custody disputes. Others are victims of crimes ranging from the stealing of someone else's child by a person who wants to be a parent, to sexual abuse, torture, and homicide. Here are some precautions to keep in mind for protecting your child.

• Never let your baby or toddler be unsurpervised in a public place even for a moment. Don't leave your child outside a store in a carriage or stroller. Never leave a child alone in a parked car, even if the car is locked.

• No matter how tempted you might be, don't let your toddler "get lost" in a department store or supermarket so you can finish shopping in peace before claiming your offspring from the store manager. Your shopping tasks might be easier without a toddler in tow, but the risk to your child's safety isn't worth it.

• Know the persons to whom you entrust your child for baby-sitting. Make sure that the baby-sitter is instructed to keep your child closely in hand in places such as the park, playground, stores, streets and sidewalks.

• Don't lull yourself into a false sense of security by thinking that crimes against children only happen in big cities or in someone else's town. Children have been molested or stolen on lawns and playgrounds in the nicest of neighborhoods. Your toddler should never be out of sight or out of mind in a place (even if the place is your own yard) where someone could approach and cause harm. Strangers are not the only risk. Some incidents involve acquaintances, familiar neighborhood faces, or even friends and relatives. A toddler does not have the judgment, understanding, or physical resources to cope with a problem involving an older unstable person. No young child should be left in an unsupervised situation where such coping might become necessary.

LEARNING AND ENJOYING

There are so many new things in a young child's world that each day is bound to contain a great number and variety of learning experiences whether or not you plan it that way. It's not necessary or even desirable to involve a toddler in formal instruction in school-related skills such as reading readiness. Nevertheless, the way you interact with your child and the early experiences you provide can pay off in successful achievement later on. Don't push or pressure your child, but do make an effort to provide positive reinforcement for his or her learning efforts.

Talking and Listening

The most useful thing you can do to help your child learn to talk is to provide lots of interesting conversation for him or her to listen to and respond to and to imitate. Here are some hints on making what you say to your child do the most good.

• Use the name labels for things. For example, say, "Here's your sweater," rather than, "Here it is."

• Address your child by name, and use the name rather than a pronoun. For example, say, "Let's find Stevie's toy," instead of, "Let's find your toy."

• Be expressive. Use gestures and intonation to help your speech hold the child's attention. It's even fine to overdo it and be a bit theatrical if you wish.

• Your child can understand far more than he or she can express at this time. Keep this in mind as you speak. Be sure to give the child credit for understanding what's going on when he or she can in fact do so. Be careful not to say things in front of your child that you don't want the child to repeat some day. Avoid saying things which might alarm the child unnecessarily. Assume that he or she will get the message even if the words to say it back are not there.

• As your child puts words together to make phrases and sentences, listen carefully. Try to understand. Don't worry about syntax which, although it is developing according to logical rules, may differ from your adult standard language. Don't correct the grammar of a toddler. It will straighten out on its own as time goes on. However, when you respond to your child's language, use your syntax, not the child's.

Learning to Listen

Take time to call your toddler's attention to different sounds in the environment, and then talk about what you hear. The ticking of a watch or clock, a dog barking, a cat purring, cars or trucks going by, an airplane passing overhead, the kettle boiling, the bath water running, a person hammering, footsteps and hands clapping are examples of sounds you could use. Try sitting (or lying down) comfortably with your child. Both close your eyes and listen. See how many sounds you can identify. At first, you'll be the one to talk about what you hear. Then, when your child gets better at listening and using language, he or she can be the one to tell you about sounds.

Encourage your child to listen to music. Share your own favorites if you wish. (Be careful, however, not to turn the volume so high that it causes fright or damaged ears!)

> Excellent suggestions for using music with babies and toddlers can be found in *Your Baby Needs Music*, by Barbara Cass-Beggs. This book contains rhymes, songs, and lullabyes presented in a way that will suit even nonmusical parents. If you can't find it in your local bookstore, *Your Baby Needs Music* can be ordered directly from the publisher, St. Martin's Press, 175 Fifth Avenue, New York, NY 10010.

Things to Smell

Help your child to notice and identify different odors in your environment. As you are cooking, take the time to let your toddler sniff at ingredients as you tell the name of each one. (Omit from this experience any powdered or finely crushed dry items which could be inhaled.)

Share with your child personal products with different aromas—after shave, cologne, hand cream, his or her own baby lotion, and similar items. (This must be a supervised activity, both for your child's safety and the products' longevity.) Use cotton balls to make a sniffing sampler for your child. Put a few drops of an interesting substance (perfume, cooking extract, fruit juice, vinegar, etc.) on each piece of cotton and let your child smell it while you talk about what it is.

"Scratch and sniff" books are fun, and they can help you provide interesting experiences to educate your toddler's sense of smell. Ask your local bookseller to recommend current titles.

Art Activities

Art activities for a toddler needn't be elaborate to be fun. Plan in advance for the inevitable mess, and let your child create and enjoy. Here are some suggestions.

• Supplies such as crayons, paints, and paste should be nontoxic. They should also be washable and of the nonpermanent variety. Items such as permanent felt tip markers or ball point pens can leave marks which will outlast a toddler's childhood, so keep such devices unavailable.

• For painting, let your child use water base poster paints. A large plastic tablecloth makes an excellent cover for the floor. One of your old shirts can serve as a full length smock. Large sheets of paper make it easier for your child to put the colors where they belong rather than on the table or walls.

• If your child is tired of painting on paper, try making painted rocks. A smooth stone painted with poster paint can become an animal, a flower, a house, or just about anything your child imagines it to be.

• Vanilla pudding (tinted with fruit juice or food coloring) makes an excellent fingerpaint which causes no harm when bits of the mess end up in the mouth.

• A chalkboard securely fastened on the wall at child height is great fun. Make sure that the only writing tools near the chalkboard are pieces of chalk. A toddler is unlikely to be able to discriminate between chalk and a crayon.

• When your child creates something, treat the product with respect. If he or she tells you it's a picture of an elephant, don't say it looks like a rock. If the random scribbles on a page are identified as a letter to grandma, there's no harm in helping the child find an envelope.

Things to Touch

As your toddler touches things (as he or she inevitably will), call attention to any significant features of each object's texture or shape. Introduce your child to the concepts of soft, hard, rough, scratchy, smooth, wet, damp, dry, squishy, cold, hot, and the like.

Soft As a Kitten, by Audean Johnson (Random House, New York: 1982) contains interesting textures for your child to touch, along with a simple text and bright illustrations, and even one "scratch and sniff" page. This title is just one example of the "touch me" books from Random House. Consult your bookstore for a complete list.

Help your child to make his or her own "touch me" book. Use heavy construction paper for the pages, and items such as fabric samples, wallpaper, sandpaper, aluminum foil, embossed greeting cards, or other textured items to paste on the pages. Be sure to use a nontoxic glue such as library paste.

Shoe Box Surprises

An ordinary shoe box can be transformed into a container for interesting items to be experienced by touch. Here's how to begin. With scissors or a sharp knife, cut two of the corners of the box (1) so the end can be pulled out to lie flat. When the box is in use, leave the top on with the end flap out so the end of the box is like an open door (2). To store the box, push the side back to its closed position, put the cover back on, and secure it all with a heavy rubber band (3).

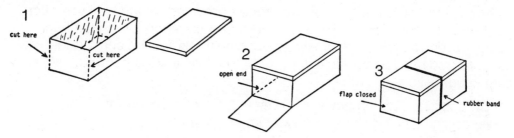

Here's how to use the shoe box for learning games with your toddler. Begin by placing two familiar objects (e.g., a model car and a tiny doll) in the box. Have your child reach in and, without looking, find the car. Talk about how the object feels. ("How can you tell it's a car?" "What do the wheels do?") Then have the child pull the object out and see if he or she is correct.

To make the game more difficult, add more objects or use objects which are not as easy to identify. To help teach your child concepts of size, shape, and texture, use objects such as a stone, a sponge, a bit of soft cloth, etc. Give the child directions such as "Find me something very hard." "Which thing in the box could you use to dry dishes?" "Pull out the biggest thing you can find."

There are many different shoe box games you can invent as you go along. The shoe boxes also make garages for small cars, barns for small animals, and anything else your child imagines them to be.

Fantasy Play

Young children often engage in play which may involve imaginary props, creative use of ordinary objects, and even imaginary animals or playmates. Respect your child's imaginative endeavors, and don't ever make fun of this fantasy world which, to a toddler, may seem very real and meaningful indeed. For example, don't think it's silliness if your child carries on a conversation using the hairbrush (or similar object) as a telephone receiver. Be sure to answer and provide *your* half of the conversation if the call is for you! Don't be disappointed if the call is not for you. Many children create imaginary playmates and involve them in complicated activities. These fantasy companions generally cause a toddler no harm, and can be lots of fun, but when a clever child begins to blame naughty behavior on the "friend," it's quite all right to introduce a bit of reality and point out that you know better.

Make toys and appropriate household objects (safe ones) available to support your child in fantasy play. A large cardboard carton, for example, may serve as a rocket to carry a toddler to the moon one minute, and a barn for imaginary horses or a hospital for sick dolls the next. An old purse, scarves, hats, and similar items can be used for dressing up. Objects which stimulate your child's creativity are better than expensive items which do it all and leave nothing to the imagination.

LEFT-HANDED CHILDREN

If your baby or toddler shows no clear preference for one hand or another, you may attempt to encourage use of the right hand by the way you offer objects to the child. However, if a pattern of preference for the left hand develops, don't fight it. Help the child become as skillful and comfortable with the preferred hand as possible. If your child is definitely left-handed, here are some suggestions.

• Be positive. Don't in any way communicate displeasure or disappointment. Don't try to make him or her switch.

• Help the child use crayons or other writing tools. Assistance with placement of paper on the desk or table may be needed. When the time comes for cutting, provide a child's pair of left-handed scissors.

• Be sure that baby-sitters, grandparents, teachers, and other caregivers know that the child is left-handed and that you intend to let him or her remain so. Make them aware that they should in no way offer negative comments or pressure the child to change.

(See Handedness, page 75)

MANNERS

Manners are best taught to a toddler by example, rather than by telling. A young child is unlikely to place a high value on being courteous and considerate if the role models in his or her immediate environment don't practice what they preach. It's possible, for example, and even easy to teach a two-year-old to say "Please" and "Thank you," but these gestures will have little meaning if everyone else in the family grabs and takes.

No matter how fine an example you set for your offspring, don't expect the child to perform to a higher level than his or her developmental stage permits. The typically horrendous table manners of a toddler, for example, are rarely bad manners at all, but are simply a case of the child's motor coordination not yet being equal to the task of eating neatly. Trying to force a toddler to hold the spoon "properly" and to eat without spilling anything is more likely to cause eating hassles than good manners. Use common sense as you guide your child through the steps of becoming a well mannered and civilized member of the family. Set a good example, but don't expect the unreasonable or the impossible.

MASTURBATION

Exploration of his or her own body is a normal and natural activity for a baby. Sooner or later, your child is going to discover the genitals and find that touching them feels pleasant. For a baby, this discovery will not be (and should not be) any more significant than locating the fingertips, toes, or any other body part. It's important that adults not introduce their own sexual feelings into the way they deal with normal infant and toddler exploration of the genitals. Remember that masturbation is not a moral issue for a toddler, who couldn't possibly understand why an adult might react so fiercely to a display of this behavior.

In most cases, the best way to deal with a young child who touches his or her genitals is to ignore the behavior. Chances are that calling attention to it will only serve to reinforce and intensify the behavior and add an unnecessary measure of anxiety and guilt. This does not mean, however, that you should encourage behavior that concerns or embarrasses you. Children must learn that certain behaviors are best kept private. Prevention by diversion is the best approach to dealing with a child who masturbates in public. A child happily engaged in doing something else will be too busy to bother.

If you feel that your child is frequently using masturbation as a comfort habit, and this concerns you or makes you uncomfortable, it's best to check with your pediatrician. It may be possible to support your child in finding another comfort habit which is more acceptable, but it's important that you do this in a way that does not increase the child's tensions and make matters worse.

MEDICATIONS

Keep all medications—those prescribed for your child as well as for you or for anyone else—out of your child's reach at all times. Don't count on childproof containers to do the job, although they tend to slow children down a bit. Keep any medications or veterinary products you have for your pets where your child can't get to them. Many veterinarians dispense medications in small paper packets or easily opened bottles, and there isn't even a childproof cap between your child and the poison.

If your child is sick enough to require medication, you should follow the advice of your physician. Here are some additional guidelines:

• Don't use one child's medication for another family member even if you think it will work. You might be right, but it's not worth the risk.

• Read the instructions carefully and follow them exactly. Follow the prescribed timing and the dosage.

• Don't administer medicine in the dark. It's too easy to make a mistake, especially if you're tired.

• As an extra safety check, read the label and the directions again before putting the medication away, to make sure you did it right.

• Never refer to capsules or tablets of any kind (even vitamins or aspirin) as candy. Medicine is medicine and should be presented as such. Don't tempt your child to view medicine as a treat. Even children's aspirin, despite its pleasant taste, can kill if taken in large enough quantity.

• Use all the medicine as prescribed or, if your physician directs you to stop using it, discard what's left over. Don't save prescriptions for another bout with the same illness unless you are specifically directed to do so.

• To dispose of medicine you don't need, flush it down the toilet or wash it down the drain. Don't toss it in the trash where a curious toddler might find it before the trash collector gets there.

See also Antibiotics, page 14; Poisoning, page 105; and Vitamin Supplements, page 144.

MEDICINE CABINET (Items to Have)

A thoughtfully stocked medicine cabinet can help you react quickly and appropriately to many minor ills and accidents as your child is growing up. Occasionally, having a particular item on hand (syrup of Ipecac, for example, in the event of certain poison ingestions) can save a life.

While it's fine to follow your instincts and use common sense in treating minor problems, you should not attempt to diagnose and treat a child's medical problems without the advice of a physician. Don't save prescription drugs from one family member's illness and apply them to a different child or problem. Certain medications have a limited shelf life, so it's important to check the expiration date even if you're sure it's the right medicine for the job. Because most prescription drugs are prescribed and provided in the correct quantity for treatment, you shouldn't have extras left over if you have followed the doctor's instructions carefully.

Here are some items it's good to have on hand in your home. Items marked with an asterisk (*) should be used on a physician's advice. Ask your doctor for recommendations of specific preparations or brand names.

Adhesive Tape
Adhesive Bandages (e.g., Band-Aids) in assorted sizes
Gauze Pads (in assorted sizes)
Sterile Cotton Balls
Nasal Aspirator (suction bulb for clearing infant's nose)
Penlight (handy for examining throat or eyes)
Heating Pad or Hot Water Bottle

Vaporizer
*Acetaminophen (e.g., Tylenol, Tempra, Liquiprin) in liquid form
*Antibacterial Ointment (for cuts and scrapes)
*Cough Syrup
*Antiseptic (e.g., iodine, mercurochrome)
*Syrup of Ipecac
Petroleum Jelly (e.g., Vaseline)
Zinc Oxide Ointment (for diaper rash)

MOTION SICKNESS

The motion of a moving vehicle soothes some young children to sleep. Many children seem completely unaffected by such motion. Some children, however, get sick. Motion sickness, while rarely a serious problem, can be especially inconvenient if you live in an area where you must frequently take your child in the car with you. If *you* used to get carsick as a child, this doesn't mean your offspring will be similarly afflicted, so don't anticipate travel trouble unnecessarily. However, if your child does prove to be one of those who gets sick in a moving vehicle, it's best to be prepared. Here are some suggestions.

• A light meal (never a heavy one) before you go, and easy-to-digest snacks such as dry crackers en route may help. Avoid large quantities of fluids, especially milk or sweet drinks. Give a thirsty child small sips of plain, cold water.

• Fresh air (a partially open window and no smoking in the car) may help prevent an attack of motion sickness. For a child who seems to be suffering, pull over in a safe place, and let the child take a few deep breaths outside the car before going on.

• For some children, the front seat of a car seems less likely to provoke a vomiting spell. Try the front for your child only if the car restraint can be used there. It's not safe for a toddler to use an adult seatbelt or to ride unrestrained in the front seat.

• Try to keep your child looking straight ahead toward the horizon rather than out the side windows. Facing backward in a moving vehicle—even in a safe seat and proper restraint.—is likely to add to motion discomfort.

• Diversionary tactics such as singing and little games may work with an older child. Don't let the child look at a book or pictures until the car has stopped. Reading in a car can cause sickness even for those who normally travel well.

• Be alert to the symptoms of impending motion sickness and try to stop the car and take remedial measures before the child becomes actively sick. Don't count on a toddler being able to tell you in time. A pale or greenish tinge to the skin, visible perspiration, drooling or watering of the mouth, and apparently unprovoked tears are signs that your child may be getting ready to throw up. A normally active and chatty toddler who becomes uncharacteristically silent may be warning you that a problem is on the way.

• Have a suitable container handy. The air sickness bags found on commercial planes are ideal. The foil lined bags used for hot takeout foods also make useful sickness containers. Your local delicatessen might be willing to donate a few to the cause. Avoid flimsy plastic bags which don't work well and are not safe around young children. If your child is going to throw up, there's nothing you can do to stop it. It's best to be prepared. Always carry a good supply of packaged wet cloths or diaper wipes for cleaning up.

• If motion sickness seems to be a severe or continuing problem, discuss this with your child's pediatrician. Medication may be helpful in some cases.

If your child is one of those who doesn't travel well, make plans to deal with the situation and try to make the best of it. Above all, don't blame the child. He or she can't help it. Clean up the mess and get on with your trip. Don't let your tension or anger make an already miserable child feel even worse.

NAPS

Are naps necessary? For most children they are. The naptime procedures you establish should be based on your child's needs and not on a rigid routine or somebody else's chart that says a child of a certain age needs a certain amount of sleep. You know your child best. Most children take at least two naps a day—one in the morning and one in the afternoon—until they are a year old or more, but some don't seem to need to.

Many children go through a difficult stage during the second year when one nap is not quite enough although two naps are too much. Be flexible. Encourage your child to take a nap if he or she seems tired, but don't force or fight over it. Most children, if given the opportunity, will take the rest they need. Some children require and thrive on a regularly scheduled nap each afternoon until school age. Others are quite able to do without any naps at all by their second year, and insisting on one causes conflict but meets no real needs (except, perhaps, the need of the caregiver for some time off).

Sometimes a child who doesn't take regular naps may just "conk out" on a given day for an hour or two. If so, let it happen. Try to be sensitive to your child's sleep needs and make provisions to meet them, even if it means temporary rearrangement of your day's plans. An exhausted child will not be good company at the supermarket or wherever else you had planned to spend the afternoon. Tired toddlers are more likely to have tantrums. Naps can be nice at times like these.

NEATNESS

Neatness is almost never a strength of a child under the age of three. The urge to use newly developing mobility and independence to explore is just not compatible with a neatly arranged environment where nothing is ever out of place. That doesn't mean you have to accept continuing chaos, however. It simply means that you must be clever about maintaining a balance between your child's need to be messy and your need for order. The trick is to accomplish this with a minimum of conflict.

Trying to make a baby or toddler eat neatly is a losing cause. Prepare for the mess and don't make the table a family battleground. Newspapers under the child's high chair or feeding table will minimize floor mopping. An enormous bib will protect the clothes. It will be quite a while until your child's manual dexterity catches up to good intensions, so there's no point in demanding polite use of table utensils. Fingers are far more effective than forks and spoons, but many a child will attempt to imitate grownups and many a spoonful of food will end up somewhere other than the mouth. Be patient.

In a very few minutes, a toddler is capable of making a room look like a tornado has recently passed through. Putting one item away before taking out the next is not something most small children can do. Instead of fighting with a child to put things away, try to set up a system in which some order is part of the fun. Large cartons can be covered with contact paper and used to store toys. Putting the things in and taking them out can be as entertaining as playing with them. A large heavy plastic tablecloth or a sheet spread out on the floor makes a suitable playing surface. When it's time to put things away, the cloth can be gathered up complete with toys, tied in a knot by the corners, and put away in a closet or behind a chair until the next time.

Being neat with a small child around requires ingenuity and tact. Making cleaning up a game will help overcome the natural contrariness of a toddler Accepting a certain amount of mess as part of the price of childrearing will eliminate a source of tension.

NIGHTMARES

It's not uncommon for toddlers to have nightmares that are vivid and terrifying enough to cause waking up sobbing with fear. These nightmares of a small child may contain monsters, frightening animals or persons, and terrifying or uncontrollable machines. A considerable part of the fright is that the child feels overwhelmed and helpless.

If your child is having a nightmare, provide comfort and support. Don't try to make light of it because at that point the nightmare is very real and threatening to the child, and he or she must be able to count on you for protection. Help the child to wake up and become calm. Physical contact is important. Hold the child securely and provide reassurance. If the child's language is sufficiently advanced, encourage talking about what happened. If not, tell the child that you understand and that you will take care of him or her.

> If your child has been troubled by nightmares with monsters, try reading and talking about the book *There's a Nightmare in My Closet*, by Martin Meyer (Dial Press, New York: 1964), if you're willing to overlook the toy gun in a few of the illustrations. In this story, a small boy confronts and gains control over his nightmare by comforting the monster and inviting it into bed with him.

NOSEBLEEDS

Nosebleeds are a common problem for many young children. Many nosebleeds are caused by picking at the nose or strenuous efforts to blow. Dry air increases the likelihood of a nosebleed.

Help a child with a nosebleed sit with the head slightly forward to minimize the swallowing of blood. Check to make sure the bleeding isn't a result of a foreign body placed in a nostril. If there isn't an object in the nose which is causing the bleeding, get right on with the job of stopping the nosebleed. Use your fingers (with gauze or a small cloth if you wish) to pinch the nose firmly so that the nostrils are pressed closed. Apply this pressure for ten minutes, to give the blood a chance to clot. If the nose is still bleeding after ten minutes, try again for fifteen minutes. (Don't keep checking on it to see how things are going. Wait the full time before looking.) If this fails, call your child's doctor for advice.

For a child who seems to have frequent nosebleeds, use a cool mist vaporizer to put additional moisture in the air. A thin coating of Vaseline petroleum jelly inside each nostril may help prevent nosebleeds.

NOSE (Care of)

Mobile babies and toddlers may try to stuff small objects into the nose. Little wads of paper fashioned from toilet tissue or napkins may also find their way into a small child's nostrils. If your child has inserted an object in his or her nose, be careful not to push the object farther in as you try to remove it. Tweezers may grab a soft object such as a paper wad. Most toddlers are unable to blow out on command without sniffing in first, so asking your child to blow an object out may cause more harm than good. Because a good sneeze may dislodge the object, a bit of pepper held under the nose might do the trick. If your efforts fail, head for the hospital emergency room or call your child's doctor.

Your child may lodge an object in the nose without your noticing it. It may even be days before you realize there is a problem. Suspect this possibility if you notice a foul smell or bloody discharge, or if your child seems to have pain in the nostrils. Medical attention will probably be required for foreign objects that have been in the nose for any period of time.

Nasal congestion in children often accompanies colds or allergies. Your pediatrician may suggest nosedrops (see Colds, page 44) or adding moisture to the air (see Vaporizers, page 142).

NUTRITION

For the first few months, milk—either from the breast or from a bottle—is the perfectly balanced diet for a baby. After that, the key to good nutrition for your child is to provide a variety of nutritious foods from which, over the course of a few days or a week, your child will be likely to consume a balanced diet.

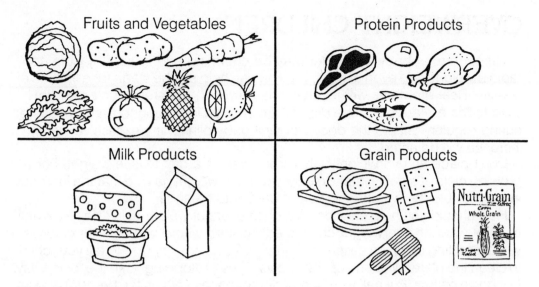

Fruits and Vegetables

Protein Products

Milk Products

Grain Products

Conscientiously trying to balance each individual meal for a toddler is an almost impossible task, and even if you set a perfectly planned and prepared meal in front of the child there would be no guarantee that all the appropriate items would end up inside. It's far better to take a slightly longer range view than one meal, and to avoid hassles. (See Feeding Problems, page 71.)

To plan a balanced diet for your child, include items from each of the four major food groups.

Milk Products (whole or lowfat milk, yogurt, cheese).

Protein Products (meat, fish, poultry, eggs, soybeans, dried peas or beans).

Fruits and Vegetables (citrus and other fruits and juices, tomatoes, leafy green vegetables, yellow vegetables, potatoes, vegetable soups and juices).

Grain Products (whole and enriched grains, cereals, breads, crackers, pasta).

Plan on approximately four servings daily for each group except protein products, in which two servings (meat and an egg, for example) will do. How big is a serving? That will vary from child to child. Here are some very general guidelines which you can adapt to your child's appetite. Two ounces of meat. A cup of milk. A slice of bread. One third to one half a cup of cooked cereal or pasta. Whatever amount of vegetable a child will consume, from a tablespoon or two to a half a cup. Do the best you can and offer variety—some of this and some of that. If you make the foods available and don't push, you can pretty much count on the child to choose wisely and eat enough. If you make a big deal out of eating specific things, you can pretty much count on having a problem.

Earl Mindell's *Vitamin Bible for Your Kids* (Bantam Books, New York: 1982) contains a wealth of nutritional information in addition to what you should know about vitamins. You might find the section entitled "Bringing Up Baby—Right!" especially helpful.

OVERWEIGHT CHILDREN

Although a fat baby or toddler may be charming and irresistibly cute, too rapid a weight gain even at this early age can help set the stage for a lifetime of obesity. Real problems with overweight, however, generally don't start until solid foods are added to the diet. When your child is weighed and measured during regular visits to the doctor or well baby clinic, any excessive weight increase will be noted.

Don't place an overweight baby or toddler on a diet to *lose* weight. For a growing child, it's best simply to slow down the weight gain so that the increase in height puts the weight and height back into balance.

How should you help slow down a child's rate of weight gain? Keep careful track of what an overweight child is eating. See where you can cut calories without cutting down on essential nutrients. Resist the impulse to tell your child to clean the plate. When he or she shows signs of stopping, take the food away. Cut down on fats. Put half as much butter (or none at all) on the bread. Try skim milk, or cut down on the total quantity of milk during a day. When your child is thirsty, offer a glass of water. Try little chunks of boiled potatoes (or mash them with skim milk) instead of french fries. Try to choose carbohydrates that provide some nutrition along with a burst of energy. If sweets and junk foods have crept into your child's diet, see if you can help them creep out. One way is simply not to buy these items for your kitchen. Provide nutritious snacks if your child seems hungry, but place a limit on the quantity. Don't let the child self-feed from bottomless bags or boxes of snack food.

If your child is overweight, cut down gradually and sensibly. Remember that your child is growing and does need a nutritious diet. Never subject a growing child to an adult fad diet. Don't try to change your child's eating habits overnight, or you might add other problems to the excess weight. Try to increase the amount of exercise your child gets each day. Work with your child's doctor to bring the weight gain back to an appropriate rate.

PACIFIERS

We recommend against the routine use of pacifiers for most babies. Don't offer a pacifier if your child is content without it.

If You Do Use One

• Use only a safe pacifier. It should be one piece — that is, the nipple, disk, and handle should be molded at one time of the same material. This is important so the baby can't disassemble it during use. The disk should be large enough so that the baby can't get the entire device into the mouth.

• Don't tie the pacifier to your baby or to the crib. A lost pacifier is preferable to a choked child.

• Don't let your baby get used to the pacifier as a device to promote sleep. Remove it when your child is drowsy. If you don't, you'll run the risk of having a child who can't go to sleep without the plug in his or her mouth. In extreme cases, a child may wake every time the pacifier falls out. This can disturb an entire household.

• Don't use the pacifier as a continuous device to deal with fussiness of all sorts. Find out what your baby needs and take care of the needs. If sucking is the need, use of the pacifier is appropriate. If you use it for every bit of fussiness, however, then the device is likely to become a comfort habit which will remain long after the strong sucking needs have passed.

• Stop using the pacifier by the time your baby is four to six months old. By this time his or her strong sucking needs will have diminished. Use of a pacifier after this will meet emotional needs other than sucking. Unless you are comfortable with pacifier use that may become a long term comfort habit for your child, take the device away before six months.

• Don't dip the pacifier in sugar, honey, or jelly. This practice may please your child and keep him or her quiet, but it's not good for the teeth or for the diet.

How to Stop

• If putting the pacifier in your baby's mouth has become a habit for *you,* stop. Make a conscious effort to offer the pacifier only when the need is there and expressed strongly. Before you offer the pacifier, see if there is anything else you can do to make the baby comfortable.

• If your baby shows any signs of rejecting the pacifier — spitting it out or not opening the mouth to take it — don't offer it unless the baby demands it and you can't comfort in any other way. Cut down gradually. Take a little longer to present it and remove it a little sooner each time.

• If gradual phasing out does not appeal to you as a technique, try stopping altogether, although this may not be easy if the pacifier has already become well entrenched as a comfort habit after strong sucking needs have passed. Tell the child that he or she can use the pacifier today, and the next day, and then no more. On the day you've chosen to stop, keep your child very busy. Encourage other comfort devices. When you make it through the first day, try for the next. If you get through three days without too much misery, you'll manage. If your child is still fiercely unhappy without the pacifier, you'll probably have to put up with its use a while longer.

• Don't try to shame your child into quitting the pacifier. Don't push the fact that the device is only for "babies" and not for children who can walk and talk. Remember, you're the one who keeps putting it in the child's mouth.

PANTS (Waterproof)

If you use disposable diapers for your baby, the plastic covering makes the use of waterproof pants unnecessary. If you use cloth diapers, you'll need waterproof pants to protect the bedclothes or the child's outer garments. No matter what you use, be sure to change the child's diapers frequently. Remember that the better the plastic pants are in protecting the clothes or bedding, the better they are at keeping the moisture inside near the baby's skin where it can cause irritating diaper rash. If you do use plastic pants for your child, make sure the elastic legs are not too tight. The pants should be a bit large rather than too small, and they should not be worn around the clock. It's best for the child if the pants permit some air to circulate and some evaporation, even though this may cause some dampness to get through.

PETS

Does your household include pet animals as well as a mobile baby or toddler? If not, your child's first two or three years are not the best time to introduce a puppy or kitten to a family that's not used to animals. If you already do have animals, there are several precautions you should take to keep your offspring and your pets healthy and happy. Young children explore by touching, and as far as a child is concerned, an animal is an object which is there to be explored. Keep this in mind, and be prepared to protect either the pet or the child, or both when needed. Here are some specific suggestions for keeping pets and children in the same house.

- Help your child learn to be kind to animals and handle them in an appropriate way. Hold the pet and show the child how to stroke it nicely. These lessons take a long time, so don't be surprised if the child tries to hold the cat by the tail with one hand while stroking it gently with the other.

- Small children and animals together need supervision. (Small children need supervision even if there aren't any animals.) While a reliable family pet is unlikely to turn on a toddler, it's not fair to either of them to permit a situation where this might occur.

- Remember that flea collars—on or off an animal—are toxic and should not be available for your child to chew on. Be sure to keep any medications for your pet out of your child's reach. As a rule, veterinary products are not dispensed in containers with childproof caps.

- Although your child will probably enjoy helping you feed and groom an animal, never make the care of a pet the responsibility of a toddler. It's not fair to either the child or the animal.

PICA

Pica (pronounced pī-ka) is the craving for unnatural foods such as sand, dirt, paint chips, plaster, or animal droppings. Although it is unusual for a person to have a desire for a regular diet of such things, it does happen. In rare cases the craving is due to a mineral deficiency in the diet. If your child seems to crave eating strange substances on a regular basis, discuss this with your pediatrician. Be especially careful that the child does not chew on painted surfaces or eat paint chips from paint that might have contained lead. Lead poisoning can cause brain damage and retardation.

Don't confuse pica with a child's normal curiosity about things. Remember that the primary tool of exploration for a mobile baby or toddler is the mouth. Most children will experiment with tasting things such as dirt or sand. A few bits in the mouth are inevitable and will usually cause no serious harm. Overreacting and making an enormous fuss if a child puts a few grains of sand in the mouth may actually help create a problem where there wasn't one before. A child who wants a parent's attention can soon learn that something forbidden in the mouth will immediately bring an abundance of attention and concern. The reaction adds considerable fascination to a bite of sand that probably wouldn't have held the child's interest without this response. Supervise and control what your child attempts to consume, but don't be theatrical about it.

PLAYPENS

Should you use a playpen for your child? Perhaps the best answer to this question is "perhaps." Read the following pros and cons of playpen use and work out the answer that best meets the particular needs of your family.

Reasons NOT to Use a Playpen

• Child can become bored during an extended playpen stay.

• Pen reduces opportunity for exploration of environment and learning from this exploration.

• Some active children do not take well to confinement.

• Because child is safe, it's easier for caregivers to ignore or delay attention to child's needs.

Reasons FOR Using a Playpen

• Playpen provides an area that is the child's own "turf." Many children find this secure and comforting.

• Use of the pen permits parents to go about necessary household chores without keeping a mobile child under constant surveillance.

• Pen makes it possible to keep a child safely in an area of the house that is not perfectly babyproofed.

• An active mobile baby or toddler can wear a parent out. Both child and parents benefit from periods of quiet play in a limited space.

• Living can't always involve total freedom, and it doesn't hurt a child to learn this fact early.

How to Use a Playpen

If you decide to use a playpen for your child, here are some guidelines to help you make it a positive experience for all of you.

• Begin using the playpen *before* your baby is mobile. A pen introduced *after* a child has started to crawl will seem like a cage for confinement, but one that's been a part of the regular routine from the beginning may not.

• Make sure your child has interesting (and safe!) toys so that time spent in the playpen won't be boring.

• If you intend to move the playpen from one place to another, choose one that's lightweight and easy to fold, but sturdy enough to remain firmly in the set-up position when in use. Sides made of very fine mesh screening are the best. The slightly larger mesh can trap tiny fingers, and anything large enough to put toes or feet into will provide a climbing ladder to the outside and defeat the entire purpose. The playpens with bars require an arm's length (and then some) safety area around them so objects don't get pulled inside.

• Don't use the playpen as punishment. Try to keep its associations pleasant. "You've been bad, so you've got to go to your pen," is a sure way to make your child dislike the playpen.

• The older your toddler gets, the more opportunities you should provide for carefully supervised activity outside the pen. Your child's energy level along with your tolerance level will work together to determine how and how rapidly you phase out using the playpen.

• Don't leave your child in the playpen for extended, uninterrupted periods of time. A few minutes of attention two or three times in an hour will do you both good. If you can, keep the playpen where the child can watch what's going on. If not, check from time to time to see what your child is doing.

POISONING

For small children, poisoning is the second most common cause of accidental death. Approximately half a million children a year require emergency medical treatment for poisoning. More than 3,000 of these children, the greatest number of them under five years old, die.

The only sure way to prevent poisoning is to keep poisonous things away from children. Infants and toddlers use their mouths as primary tools for exploration. A curious child may consume something even if it tastes awful. Children have been known to drink (and be killed by) entire containers of paint remover, bleach, liquid detergent, and similar substances that would hardly seem to compete with milk or juice for palatability. Research tells us clearly that toddlers are not put off by the dreadful taste of a substance. We know personally of one toddler (son of a physician) who consumed a diaper pail deodorizer at a friend's house and then told his mother "Cookie taste yucky."

Bad as the item tasted, the child ate it first and complained later. Fortunately, the alert mother (a nurse) identified the object eaten, called the Poison Control Center, and got advice in time. Because she had syrup of Ipecac on hand, she was able to administer the directed treatment immediately. The child vomited up the "yucky cookie" and no harm was done. Knowing where to call and being able to follow the directions on the spot saved valuable minutes and perhaps the child's life.

Always keep poisonous substances in their original containers. Never use soda bottles or mason jars to store household products. It's dangerous to make a poisonous substance more appealing by putting it in a friendly container. And, if your child should eat something harmful, it's essential to be able to identify the exact substance immediately, and you will need the label of the product in order to do this.

As an additional precaution, let your toddler help you put *Mr. Yuk* labels on poisonous materials. Instruct your child never to touch or taste anything with a *Mr. Yuk* picture on it. If you use *Mr. Yuk* labels as a poison prevention technique, it's absolutely essential that you use the labels only as directed. Your child will not take the labels seriously if they appear as frivolous decorations on objects that are not poisonous. The toddler who sees *Mr. Yuk* on your coffee mug or the refrigerator door may miss the entire point when he or she finds the same sticker on the dishwashing detergent.

Mr. Yuk is the poison warning symbol of the National Poison Center Network, Children's Hospital of Pittsburgh.

The National Poison Center Network has developed excellent materials for teaching poison prevention to young children at home. Their *Under 5 Understanding Cards* can be used to teach children about different kinds of poison and what the *Mr. Yuk* stickers mean. The front of each card has an illustration, and the other side contains teaching suggestions and a brief script for the parent or other caregiver to use while teaching the child what the illustration represents.

> *Mr. Yuk* stickers (20 for $1.00) and the *Under 5 Cards* ($2.00 per set) can be ordered directly from
>
> **The National Poison Center Network**
> Children's Hospital of Pittsburgh
> 125 DeSoto Street
> Pittsburgh, PA 15213
>
> In many areas these materials can be obtained from the local Poison Control Center or your pediatrician.

Obtain the number of your nearest Poison Control Center. Write it in a safe place near your telephone. (A sticky label right on the phone is best. Use a *Mr. Yuk* label if you wish. Be sure it's fastened securely so that your toddler can't peel it off. The telephone is the one exception to the rule that you should put *Mr. Yuk* labels only on containers of poison. As an added bonus, *Mr. Yuk* might deter your toddler from playing with the telephone.) Most doctors prefer that you call the Poison Control Center directly to save time. Ask your child's pediatrician whom you should call first in case of a poisoning emergency.

Keep syrup of Ipecac available in case you need it to make your child vomit. You can get it in any pharmacy. However, you shouldn't use it unless a physician or the Poison Control Center tells you to. Some poisonous substances can cause almost as much harm coming up as they did going down. Have a can of activated charcoal on hand for diluting poisons in case you are directed to do so by the Poison Control Center. You can buy activated charcoal in most pharmacies or health food stores.

If your child swallows something poisonous, here's what to do:

(1) Call the Poison Control Center (or your physician) immediately. Have the container in hand so you can describe exactly what the child has taken. You will be told what to do next. If you act promptly, many poisoning emergencies can be handled at home.

(2) If you can't reach the Poison Control Center or a physician, get your child to the emergency room of the nearest hospital as fast as you can. Take along the container from which the child ate or drank. If the child has vomited, take the vomitus for analysis as well.

PUNISHMENT

It's important for parents of young children to understand the difference between punishment and discipline. Discipline involves the structure that you set up for the child's behavior—the rules you expect to be followed. Punishment is not the structure, but the penalty for violating that structure.

Every child, no matter what the age, needs discipline. Predictable rules of family life are essential for civilized living and are an important part of a child's security as well. Punishment, on the other hand, should not be an issue in the case of a baby or toddler because children that young are not yet able to understand the cause and effect relationship between something they have done and some punishment that follows. Instead of contributing to discipline, frequent punishment of a very young child is likely to confuse the matter.

Aggressive behavior toward a child (e.g. hitting or biting a child for some transgression) brings with the punishment an example of behavior you don't want to encourage. Punishments such as withholding a treat or even confining the child to a quiet corner just don't have the intended effect with a child who is still too young to connect these consequences with his or her own behavior.

With a baby or toddler, the best way to deal with punishment is to prevent the need for it as often as you can. Remove your child from a troublesome situation *before* something goes wrong. For example, put away the china teacups before one gets dropped on the kitchen floor. Don't leave your toddler alone with the cat long enough to put it in the dishwaster and then try to retrieve the animal tail first.

When a small child starts to do something he or she shouldn't (hit a playmate or crayon on the wall, for example) stop him or her quickly, calmly, and firmly. The word, "NO!" and a brief comment can, with the right tone of voice, communicate all the anger and displeasure needed.

(See also Curiosity, page 50; Discipline, page 57; and Spanking, page 120.)

QUARANTINE

Should you keep a child with a contagious disease away from other people? If so, for how long? It's generally a good idea to keep a contagious child isolated for awhile so that others who haven't had the disease won't catch it. Of course, anyone who came in contact with the child just before you knew that he or she was sick was probably already exposed, and your precautions might be too late. Nevertheless, it's best to try. An additional reason for keeping a sick child away from others is to prevent that child from acquiring new germs from friends who might be in the early stages of something. Why complicate matters? Let the child get rid of one disease before coming down with another.

If your child has a disease that's not especially serious in a young child but is potentially harmful to others, it's only fair to be very careful not to put others at risk. For example, a child with rubella (German measles) should be isolated until the danger of exposing a pregnant woman to rubella has passed. While rubella is usually a mild disease in a child, a mother who contracts it during pregnancy may give birth to a child with severe defects. Another example is a child with mumps, who should be kept away from teenage boys or men who haven't had the disease. A bad case of mumps can cause a man to become sterile.

Of course, if you follow the prescribed schedule of innoculations (see Immunizations, page 84), you're less likely to have to worry about quarantine because there will be a number of childhood diseases that will simply pass your child by.

It's very difficult to quarantine a child with a cold effectively. By the time you realize that your child has a cold, he or she has probably given it to any other children around anyway. Toddlers seem to pass colds from one to the other and back again no matter what you try to do about it. (See Colds, page 44.) Be reassured that as your child gets older and develops more immunity, he or she will have fewer colds.

REYE'S SYNDROME

Reye's syndrome is a rare, but serious and sometimes fatal, disease that may follow a virus infection in a child such as influenza or chicken pox. Some recent research has suggested a possible relationship between Reye's syndrome and use of aspirin in treating a child with the flu. Even though very few children who take aspirin develop Reye's syndrome, most pediatricians are now extremely cautious about using aspirin to deal with a child's cold or flu symptoms. If your child seems to have the flu, it's best to consult with the doctor. Don't administer doses of aspirin on your own. Feel free to ask your doctor whatever questions you might have about this matter.

Reye's syndrome is a very rare disease, and chances are you will never need to worry about it. However, because Reye's syndrome can kill a child so quickly, parents should be aware of its symptoms so that they can get help immediately if the need arises. If your child has a viral infection (influenza, cold, chicken pox) be alert to the following, especially during the recovery period:

- vomiting, especially if it's persistent

- lethargy (unusual lack of energy)

- strange or unusual behavior or personality change (a child who isn't himself or herself)

Don't be afraid to call your child's doctor if you are concerned about any or all of the above symptoms. If you are unable to reach the doctor immediately, take your child to the nearest emergency room. In case the problem is Reye's syndrome, prompt treatment is essential. If it isn't Reye's syndrome, no harm will have been done. It's better to be safe than sorry.

ROUGH PLAY

Avoid the temptation to shake and toss your baby or toddler around even in fun. Too much roughhousing can get out of hand, cause anxiety, and possibly cause physical injury. Do have fun playing with your child, but never forget that he or she is no match for you in size, strength, or ability to sort out the teasing from the reality. When the fooling around begins to border on violence, you've gone much too far.

SAFETY GATES

Safety gates can be used to close off places you don't want your mobile baby or toddler to explore. A gate in a doorway can keep a child out of a room that isn't childproof. If your house has more than one floor, a gate at the top of the stairs and another one at the bottom is a must. Gates are not a substitute for supervision, and you should not assume that a gate will do the entire job of keeping your child where he or she belongs. What a gate will do, however, is reduce the chances of a problem, although you should keep in mind that the gate itself may present a hazard under certain circumstances.

There are two types of safety gates you can purchase. One, which opens and folds like an accordion, is available for permanent installation or with a pressure bar. The second type is a portable mesh gate which is kept in place by a pressure bar.

A permanently installed gate is easier for an adult to open and close once it's in place. The pressure bar gates can be irritating to replace every time you want to go in and out of a room. Pressure bar gates can be pushed out of place, and they are especially unsuited for the top of a staircase. The accordion type folding gates, on the other hand, have been known to trap the head of a toddler trying to climb over and cause serious injury or death. These gates provide a foothold for a climbing child, and it's unwise to leave a child unattended and depend on the gate to do the entire job. (The accordion type folding play yards present the same hazard, and children should not be left in them without supervision.) If not fastened securely, these folding devices can fold up and pinch small fingers and hands.

Whichever type of gate you choose, keep in mind that it's an aid to protecting your child but not a panacea. A mobile baby or toddler must still have an adult in the vicinity to ensure safety.

SAFETY HARNESSES

A safety harness can be a valuable barrier between a mobile baby or toddler and an accident about to happen. Use a safety harness to keep your child secure in the high chair, the carriage, or the stroller. If you have just one harness and try to use it for everything, there may be a day you'll be too busy to switch it from the high chair to the carriage or vice versa. That's likely to be the day your child makes a headfirst exit from where he or she is supposed to be. The cost of two or three harnesses still doesn't come close to the cost of one visit to the emergency room. It's best to have a harness handy for each piece of equipment your child uses regularly.

A safety harness with horse reins attached is extremely useful when you take an active toddler for a walk anywhere it wouldn't be safe for the child to run about. With the harness, your child will have a bit of room for exploring, but you can rein him or her in before you reach the next street to cross, the gap in the fence near the nasty dog, or the glittering piece of broken glass that beckons a small hand to clutch it. Using the reins is easier than trying to keep hold of the hand of a toddler who's intent on darting this way or that.

Use a safety harness to keep your child safe in a situation where he or she could fall or dash away even though you are right there. Don't use a harness to confine your child for any period of time while you are not watching. You wouldn't want to come back and find your child suspended upsidedown in the harness somewhere between the seat and the floor. Never use a harness to attach your child to a tree or fence in the yard. When your child is out playing, you should be out there too.

If your toddler has taken to leaving the crib at night, don't use a harness as the means to keep him or her in. Find a better way to deal with sleep problems.

SALT (Sodium)

Sodium is a mineral occurring naturally in many foods. It is also used in certain preservatives and flavor enhancers. Table salt is 40% sodium. While it is true that a child needs a certain amount of sodium for normal growth and development, it is also true that a typical infant diet (milk and baby food) contains more sodium than a child requires. An excess of sodium is not only unnecesssary, but potentially harmful. Too much sodium in the diet may eventually contribute to the development of high blood pressure.

If you feed your child from the family table, remove his or her portion before adding salt. (Cutting down on salt will be better for all of you. Experiment with alternative flavorings such as herbs or lemon.) Commercial baby foods are now manufactured with no salt added because they are better for your baby that way. Do not add salt to your baby's food to please your own taste. Keep in mind that your child doesn't find the bland taste of baby food as boring as you do, and it's just as well if he or she never acquires a taste for salty things.

SEPARATION ANXIETY

During much of your child's second and third year, his or her life will involve conflict between the striving for independence and the fear of being separated from you. The typical toddler is very ambivalent about his or her emerging independence—fighting for it one moment and turning full circle to clinging dependency the next—which can be very disconcerting to caregivers. It's not unusual for a toddler to cry vigorously when left at a playground or day-care center (even one where he or she is normally very content) and then an hour or two later to resist going home again.

Understand that fear of separation from you is an essential and inevitable part of your child's efforts to work out his or her independence as a person, and that there will be struggles no matter how predictable, secure, and supportive you are in dealing with this. Here are some suggestions to help you keep separation anxiety to a healthy minimum.

• Right from the start, if you are going to leave your child with a babysitter, be honest about it. Don't sneak off after bedtime and hope your child will sleep through your absence and not notice you were gone. Avoid creating a situation in which a child might wake up to find someone else in your place, an event which is likely to result in lack of trust, extreme fear of separation, and sleeping problems. It's better to leave when the child is awake and to reassure him or her that you will return.

• Be firm and matter of fact about leaving your child when it's necessary. If you work and use a day-care center, tell your child the truth. Don't say you'll be in the next room or across the street if you won't. Don't promise to be back in a few minutes if you're going to be gone all day. Reassure the child that you will be back before supper, or after naptime, or whenever. Use a reference point that the child can relate to. Then keep your word.

• Separation at bedtime is an important part of developing independence. Careful attention to predictable bedtime rituals can help your child feel secure. For a child who has trouble separating at bedtime, frequent but brief reassurances that you are in the house are helpful.

• Be sensitive to well intentioned but silly comments from acquaintances or strangers that might frighten your child. The neighbor or shopkeeper who says,"You're so cute I'd like to take you home with me," means no harm, but such remarks can throughly alarm a small child. Say firmly that your child is coming home with *you,* and leave no doubt in the child's mind that this is so.

SEX EDUCATION

Sooner or later your child will ask questions about where babies come from and about the differences between girls and boys. How you handle these questions may have considerable influence on your child's feelings about sexuality and his or her sense of self as a sexual being. Here are some suggestions for dealing with this very sensitive and personal subject.

• Answer the question asked, but don't provide more information than the child requires or can handle at that time. For example, the toddler who asks if a baby really grows inside a mommy can be told, "Yes, there's a special place there for the baby to stay until it's time to be born." A lecture complete with diagrams on all the facts of reproduction is not what the child is seeking at this point. (You've probably heard at least one version of the anecdote in which a parent launches anxiously into the long prepared speech on human reproduction only to be interrupted by an impatient child saying, "But Jenny came from Kansas.")

> An excellent book for parents to read is *Talking with Your Child about Sex: Questions and Answers for Children from Birth to Puberty,* by Dr. Mary S. Calderone and Dr. James W. Ramey (Random House, New York: 1982). The material in this book, in question and answer format, can help you develop an open and comfortable approach to handling your child's questions. The book is frank and direct, and it counsels parents to be well-informed and honest with their children.

• If your child asks, be sure to explain that he or she is constructed normally. The girl who wonders why her brother has a penis and she doesn't should be reassured that she isn't broken or defective, and that the way she is made will enable her to have a baby when she grows up. The little boy who asks why he doesn't have breasts like his mother can be told that grownup women have breasts so they can feed their babies, and that men and boys do have nipples and breasts which are flat because they don't need them to feed babies.

• Be honest with your child. Don't make up stories you'll have to undo later. Babies are not purchased at department stores or hospitals, found under cabbage leaves, or brought by storks. Such tales serve no purpose.

> A lovely book to read to a preschool child is *Where Do Babies Come From?*, by Margaret Sheffield, with illustrations by Sheila Bewley (Alfred A. Knopf, New York: 1981). Using simple words and beautifully sensitive pictures, the story of conception, prenatal development, and birth is told in a loving, honest, and gentle way. In these days of amniocentesis, you might wish to omit the sentence "It's impossible to tell whether a baby is a boy or a girl while it is still in the womb." Other than this minor flaw, the book is very sound and well worth having.

• Use the correct words for body parts. The words *penis* and *vagina* or *vulva* are not "naughty" words unless you make them so. These labels should be used in as matter of fact a way as words like *toes, tummy*, or *knees.*

• Accept the fact that even very young children are sexual beings. Your baby or toddler will have a natural and healthy curiosity about his or her own body. A child soon learns that touching himself or herself feels good. Even if your upbringing has caused you to feel shameful or embarrassed about sexuality, try not to communicate these discomforts to your child. This does not mean, however, that you should encourage or permit your child to masturbate in public or engage in exploratory play with other young children. This is an area of behavior in which limits are appropriate and limits must be set. What's important is to set the limits in a way that does not make the child feel guilty or shameful about his or her body or feelings. (See Masturbation, page 93.)

SEX ROLES

The sex role stereotypes which have been part of our society for many generations die hard, even when conscious efforts are made to eliminate them. Whether or not they intend to do so, most parents do seem to treat boys and girls differently although these differences may be subtle. As you rear your child, you have to be who you are and do what's comfortable for you as a family. You should try, however, to eliminate harmful and unnecessary

sex role stereotyping from your child's life as much as you can.

Boys and girls do have some basic differences (obviously and thank goodness!). What should not be different, however, is the opportunity provided for each child to develop fully as a person. No part of the wide range of opportunity to achieve or to express oneself should be denied a person simply on the basis of whether that person is male or female. Boys should be encouraged to express their emotions and be gentle, tender, and kind. Girls can enjoy and participate in active play and romping about. Boys can play with dolls and girls with model cars. Everybody can wear bright colors and nobody need wear only pink or only blue. Both boys and girls can dream of growing up to be doctors, firefighters, baseball players, horse trainers, chefs, clothes designers, teachers, nurses, scientists, homemakers, artists, writers, or anything else they wish to be. Don't prejudge and force your child into a mold that meets your expectations rather than the child's talents and needs.

In your efforts to avoid sex role stereotyping, there's no need to go overboard and forbid toys or clothes which traditionally have applied to one sex or the other. For example, if your little girl doesn't want to play with trucks or a tool set she shouldn't have to. It's as appropriate for a girl to aspire to be a wife and mother as it is for her to hope to be a doctor. Don't force baby dolls on a little boy who will have no part of them. The tender nurturing feelings about small creatures can be developed in other ways. Use common sense and do what's comfortable for you and your children.

SHAMPOOS

It will be necessary to wash your child's hair from time to time. This may not be easy. Water poured on the head frightens some children. Soap in the eyes only makes matters worse. Here are some suggestions.

• If your child is fearful, don't make hairwashing part of the regular bath. If you do, you're likely to end up with fears of baths *and* shampoos, not an easier shampoo.

• Don't pour water to wet the hair. Apply water and then shampoo with a wet washcloth. Use a non-sting shampoo (such as Johnson's Baby Shampoo) and just enough water to do the job, but not enough to create the sensation of running water. Rinse with a clean washcloth or sponge dipped again and again into clear water. This will cause fewer problems than pouring.

• A plastic headband or shampoo shield may help keep water off the face. Using such a device may even make it possible to pour the water. A dry towel held over the child's eyes may do the trick if you don't have a shampoo shield.

• Some children like a blow dryer. Others are frightened by it. A dryer is handy if your child will tolerate it. If not, towel dry the hair and then comb or brush it. Use a wide toothed comb. Be gentle with the tangles.

• For an older toddler you might try playing "beauty salon." Make an appointment for your child to have a shampoo. Set out all the "equipment" and make a big deal about it. You can use this as an excuse for a manicure as well.

Not all children require special efforts for successful hairwashing. Some children even enjoy a shampoo. Perhaps you'll be lucky.

SHOES AND SOCKS

It's fine to let your baby do without shoes until he or she is walking outside, when shoes are needed to protect the feet from a world that isn't always nice for walking.

• Shoes should be large enough to give the feet room to develop. Too large is better than too small, but shoes should never be so large that the child curls toes or contorts the foot to keep the shoes on.

• It's best to have shoes professionally fitted in a reliable store and checked for size at least every three months. Shoes must be the correct width and length, and a new pair should have one-half to three-quarters of an inch growing room beyond the longest toe.

• Shoes should be flexible rather than stiff with firm support. A child's foot must be able to move freely to develop strength.

• Don't keep a pair of shoes that doesn't fit, even for special occasions. Comfortable, everyday shoes are better for party wear than dressy shoes which are too tight. Don't count on your child to tell you if shoes are too small. A toddler's feet are so flexible that they will crush to fit the space, and damage could be done without the child feeling pain.

• Flat soles with nonskid surface that may keep a child from slipping and falling are best. Avoid strangely shaped shoes, shoes with heels, and novelty items such as cowboy boots for a toddler. Dressy shoes for a toddler are an unnecessary expense, and your child probably won't get enough wear out of a pair to justify the purchase.

• Don't pass used shoes on to other children, even if the shoes look brand new. A young child's feet are so flexible that they mold to fit the shoes, and shoes that have "broken in" to someone else's foot could cause a problem even if they appear to be the correct size.

• Socks that are too small can cause harm just as tight shoes can. Make sure your child's socks give the toes plenty of room. Cotton socks are good because they let the feet "breathe," but be careful not to shrink them in the laundry. Get rid of outgrown socks so you won't use them by mistake. If you buy several pairs of socks that look alike, you'll still find some that match when half of each pair disappears (as socks inevitably do).

SIBLING RIVALRY

As long as there have been brothers and sisters, there has been sibling rivalry. Some competition and feelings of resentment and jealousy should be anticipated and not cause undue concern. Try to treat all your children with understanding, and make efforts to see that sibling rivalry doesn't get out of hand and escalate into something more resembling hate.

New Baby in the Family

The arrival of a new baby can be an exciting and wonderful event. It can also be a source of jealousy and unhappiness for your toddler who isn't ready to give up his or her place for a new arrival.

• Let your toddler help you prepare for the baby's arrival. Let him or her share in the shopping and getting the crib or room ready. (It's unwise, however, to make the toddler give up his or her own crib at this time. Make a different arrangement for the baby if you can.)

• Prepare your toddler in advance for the fact that you will be going to the hospital to have the baby (unless, of course, you plan to deliver at home). Some hospitals permit sibling visits to the nursery. Take advantage of this opportunity if it's available.

• The day you bring your new baby home, go out of your way to pay special attention to your toddler. (Think how difficult it must be for a child to sit unnoticed while everyone fusses over the new baby. Make sure this doesn't happen in your family.)

• Plan some time each day to do something personal and special with your toddler, and give him or her your undivided attention at this time. The time need not be long, but it must be something the child can count on. For example, while the baby naps you could read a story, play a game, or make something. Have a conversation with your child. Listen to what he or she has to say.

• A toddler who sees how much attention a helpless newborn gets may try acting like a baby again. This is common, but you needn't indulge your child's desires. An older sibling need not return to diapers or be permitted to suck at the breast. Don't reward or punish infantile behavior, but simply ignore it. Divert the older child's attention to something appropriate for his or her age. Call positive attention to things which make the older child different from the baby. ("Thank you for picking up your toys." "Would you and Daddy like to have your juice in the new green mugs today?" "I like the way you put on your shirt.")

> Read *A Baby Sister for Francis*, by Russell Hoban (Harper & Row, New York: 1964) to a toddler with a new baby in the house.

Your Toddler and Older Children

It's best not to make your toddler a burden for your older children. While older siblings might enjoy helping care for a younger brother or sister, it's not fair to deprive an older child of his or her own childhood. Let an older child help you, but don't make care of a toddler a sibling's responsibility.

Be careful not to let your toddler do things which are suitable for an older child but not safe for a toddler. Be alert to the possibility that an older child might try to engage the toddler in unsuitable or dangerous activities. Keep your older child's toys out of a toddlers hands, both for safety reasons and because the older child should be able to enjoy some personal property without having it demolished by a two-year-old.

SINGLE PARENTS

A single person can be a capable, successful parent, and the child of a single parent can develop as a happy, healthy, secure and fulfilled person. Having two parents in the home is no guarantee that all will be well. Rearing a child on your own does not necessarily mean that you or the child will suffer as a result. There are plusses and minuses to every type of family setup. Making the best of what you have is certainly preferable to using up energy lamenting the absence of a partner with whom to share the burdens (or joys). The neverending tasks of childrearing may from time to time seem overwhelming if you're on your own, but many two-parent families experience a similar sense of exhaustion and frustration.

Single parent families differ greatly from one to another as do two-parent families. There is no particular piece of advice uniquely suited to a single parent situation. All human beings—parents with or without partners, and their children—need security, a sense of belonging, and love. The specific how-to's of childcare presented in *Talk & Toddle* are for single parents, parents together, and other caregivers. The support system—extended family, friends, institutions—which you work out to meet your needs may or may not fit other people's expectations for what family life is or should be. It doesn't matter. Just do the best you can for you and your child.

SKIN CARE

For most babies and toddlers, ensuring adequate cleanliness is all the skin care required. No special efforts or fussing are necessary for most children. If there is some special or unusual problem with your child's skin, however, you should consult your pediatrician for advice. (See also Baths, page 21; Diaper Rash, page 56; Eczema, page 63; Heat Rash, page 78; and Sunburn, page 122.)

SLEEP PROBLEMS

Sleep problems are not uncommon among babies and toddlers, and how you handle these problems may well determine whether or not *you* end up with sleep problems too.

Problems at Bedtime

Many children find winding down at the end of the day difficult. Add normal toddler separation anxiety to reluctance to stop the day's activities, and you have a sleep problem in the making. Here are some suggestions.

• An overtired and tense child is often more difficult to put to bed. For the child who tends to balk at bedtime, an extra hour or so of activity is not usually the answer unless the child is clearly not tired. Avoid letting your child get overtired, even if that means an extra nap or earlier bedtime.

• Establish and pay careful attention to a routine of bedtime rituals. These predictable little routines—whichever ones you use—give your child a sense of security along with a clear signal of what you expect him or her to do in the immediate future. Bedtime should not involve surprises. Bedtime rituals such as a story enable you to give some special attention to your child while helping him or her to relax.

• Encourage the use of a comfort device such as a cuddly toy. The child who has a favorite and huggable stuffed creature in the crib may feel less alone. Involve the cuddly in the bedtime rituals. (For example, say goodnight to it and tuck it in.)

• When the bedtime rituals are completed, and the goodnights said, you should leave the room. Reassure the child that you'll be there if necessary, but that it's time for him or her to go to sleep.

• If your child cries or screams after you leave, reappear long enough to say that you are still there but it's sleep time. (Attend to any genuine needs such as changing a wet diaper or adding another blanket in a too cool room.) Don't fall for the one more drink of water game. As necessary, reappear briefly every few minutes. Stay long enough for your child to see that you're available, but no longer. You may have to do this many times for several nights, but don't give up. Sooner or later your child will believe that you won't abandon him or her (you *do* show up) and also that he or she will be left in bed because you won't permit otherwise. This is the goal: a secure, comfortable child who realizes that bedtime is inevitable. (This procedure won't work if you weaken and let the child get up to play. Once bedtime has come and the bedtime rituals have been completed, it's best to leave it so.)

Waking at Night

If your child starts waking at night, try to identify and remedy the reason. For example, is he or she cold or wet? Is the room noisy? Has there been some tension during the day? Sometimes the cause of night waking will not be easy to find. Changing a diaper is simple. Figuring out what is going on in a small person's mind and feelings may not be so easy. Try.

118

A nightmare can waken and greatly distress a toddler. If it does, provide comfort. (See Nightmares, page 97.)

The faster you attend to a child's needs when he or she wakes in the night, the sooner there's a chance you all can get back to sleep. If the child refuses to let you go, employ the same brief appearance schedule suggested for dealing with bedtime problems. Show your face, tell the child it's time to sleep, and leave. Do this as often as necessary. Letting the child "cry it out" is almost never a satisfactory solution.

Early Rising

If your child wakes long before you think it's time to start the day, a quick change of diaper or visit to the potty may make him or her comfortable enough to settle down for a while longer. A supply of toys to play with may keep a child occupied while you get a little more sleep. If you have an older child, perhaps he or she could be enticed to make early morning a togetherness time with your toddler.

Climbing Out of the Crib

When your child learns to leave the crib without your help, you must make provisions for his or her safety during and after the exit. Lower the crib side so there will be less distance to fall. You may need to try a mattress on the floor. (See page 25.) Childproof the room. Use a gate in the doorway if you wish, but respond to a child at the gate before he or she tries to climb over that. If your night wanderer gets to your room, put him or her gently but firmly back where he or she belongs.

SMOKE DETECTORS

Approximately 8,000 people die each year in home fires in the United States while another 200,000 are injured. More than 75% of the injuries and deaths from fires in the home are caused by smoke or toxic fumes. Because young children are especially vulnerable to these hazards, a smoke detector in or near the room where your child sleeps is an excellent investment in your family's safety. A good smoke detector can alert you to the presence of smoke in time to remove yourself and your child from danger before any injury occurs. A smoke alarm in every home would save many lives. Be sure to check and replace the batteries in your smoke detector at regular intervals so that the device will work as it should in time of need. (See Fire, page 73.)

SMOKING

If you smoke, you are probably well aware that smoking is harmful to your own health. The ill effects, however, do not stop with the person who smokes. A child growing up in a home where one or both parents smoke is more likely to suffer from respiratory illness than a child of nonsmokers. Your child's lungs are likely to function less well if there is smoking in your home. In addition to the direct effect a parent's smoking has on a child's health, parents who smoke set their children a bad example as well.

There is now a considerable amount of evidence that cigarette smoke harms not only those who smoke, but those close to them as well. If you smoke and have been unable to stop for your own sake, the health of your child is one more compelling reason to try again to stop. (Careless smoking is a major cause of fires in the home, and this is another risk to your child's safety that you can reduce by giving up cigarettes.) You'll be doing your child's health a favor if the

"No Smoking" rule extends to baby-sitters and other caregivers, friends, relatives, and visitors. It is becoming increasingly acceptable socially to request that people refrain from smoking, and you have every right to do so in your own home if you wish.

If you are unable or unwilling to quit smoking, it's best if you don't smoke in the room with your child. Clear the air in a room where you have just smoked before your child joins you there.

SPANKING

Should you spank or hit your child? No matter how many times you may hear it said, "Spare the rod and spoil the child"—as this expression is commonly understood—is likely to be bad advice. Physical punishment will not ensure that your child learns the specific lesson you have in mind. It may, however, convey the undesirable message that hitting people is acceptable behavior.

An infant or toddler is unlikely to be capable of making the cause and effect connection between something he or she has just done and the spanking that follows. So, even if you feel that you are dishing out a well-deserved dose of discipline, chances are that spanking will not achieve the long-term results you want. This does not mean that you should permit your child to be naughty or to do whatever he or she pleases. We are simply suggesting that there are better ways to manage a child's behavior than by using physical force. (See Discipline, page 57; and Punishment, page 107.

At one time or another, even the most even-tempered and well-meaning parent may strike a child—either as a result of accumulated exasperation or in spontaneous response to a specific situation. As long as this is not a frequent occurrence, there's no need to spend time feeling guilty about it. An occasional slap on a small hand about to throw a toy at the family dog or the television screen is hardly cause for concern. If, however, you find that striking your child or losing your temper with him or her is becoming a routine, discuss this with your family doctor, who may be able to help you find more satisfactory ways of coping with punishment. (See Child Abuse, page 39.)

STROLLERS

An umbrella-type stroller is an extremely handy item. When not being wheeled with your child in it, a stroller will fold up to fit in a car trunk, a closet, or over your arm to be instantly ready at the next moment of need.

Strollers come in many different levels of sturdiness and quality, with a wide price range to match. The one you buy should suit your particular needs and lifestyle. Stronger and more costly isn't necessarily better, although it might be. Here are some points to consider before you buy.

• Try before you buy. Make sure your choice is easy to unfold, fold, and carry. It should have a strong safety strap to contain an active child.

• Swivel wheels, at least in the front, make the stroller much easier to steer.

• If you expect to be out a lot in bad weather, consider the type with a protective enclosure that fastens on and zips up to protect your child from the elements.

STUTTERING OR STAMMERING

As a child's speech is developing, some repetition of sounds, hesitations, or even long pauses because the right word just isn't there should be considered normal. Fluency takes time to develop, and few preschool age children will speak perfectly smoothly. The greater the fuss you make about the way your child speaks, the greater the chance of causing a problem where there might not have been one. Efforts to prevent stuttering and stammering—well intentioned as these efforts might be—often reinforce the child's tendency to speech problems and insure that problems will continue.

There are likely to be occasions when your child wants to say something but the words, unable to keep up with the thoughts, stumble or tumble out not quite right. Try to listen to the content of what your child is saying, not the specific techniques of forming and putting together the words. Don't continually correct your child's efforts to communicate, and be careful not to make him or her self-conscious about speech. If you are concerned about your child's speech development, consult your pediatrician for advice. Chances are, time, patience, understanding, and a conscious effort on your part not to pressure your child will be all the remedy that's needed. If there is a problem requiring further assistance, the doctor can refer you to a qualified speech therapist.

SUGAR

Most children in the United States consume far more sugar than is needed or good for them. Even if parents make an effort to avoid the obvious sources of sugar, the typical American diet contains many sweet substances that are not so readily identifiable. It's not just sweet desserts that contain sugar. You'll find sugar in products ranging from toothpaste to ketchup and peanut butter. Children's chewable vitamins and a number of breakfast cereals aimed directly at the child market contain sugar as a major ingredient.

Why should excess sugar be avoided in your child's diet? Sugar can contribute to obesity and tooth decay. In some children, excessive sugar consumption seems to be related to hyperactivity. Too much sugar in the diet can take the place of other more needed nutrients.

For most children it's not necessary to eliminate sugar from the diet completely, and you'd probably find it difficult to do even if you wanted to. Awareness of the many ways sugar is used in today's foods will enable you to plan your child's diet sensibly so that an excess of sugar with its attendant problems can be avoided. (See also Candy and Sweets, page 35.)

• When you first introduce solid foods to your child, avoid the temptation to add a little sugar to make things "taste better." It's best to get your child accustomed to the natural taste of things.

• Not all sugar is called "sugar." Watch for ingredients the names of which end in -ose, such as fructose or dextrose. These are sugars too. Honey, molasses, maple syrup, and corn syrup are also sugars. Brown sugar is still sugar; it has molasses added to it.

• Read product labels carefully. Remember that ingredients are listed in order of importance. Be alert for and try to pass by items in which sugar plays a major role.

• Stay away from pre-sweetened cereals, sugared vitamins, and highly sweetened drinks such as Kool-Aid. (Many of these contain artificial colors as well as too much sugar.)

• Don't fall into the trap of using candy or desserts as behavior management devices. Using sweets as bribes gives them even more appeal than they normally would have.

SUNBURN

Direct exposure to the sun for any extended period of time can be a problem for babies and toddlers, whose tender skin is especially sensitive to the ultraviolet rays that cause sunburn. How long you can permit an uncovered baby or toddler to remain in the sun depends, of course, on the season, the time of day, where you live, and what the day's weather is like. Three minutes of midday summer sun on a hot day may be far too much. An hour or two of late afternoon sunshine on a spring or fall day might be pleasant and harmless.

Use common sense and some extra caution when planning sunny outings for your child. Increase periods of exposure very gradually. Start slowly, just a few minutes at first. As your child develops a protective tan, you can stay out longer.

Sunburn Prevention

• Keep in mind that a sunburn doesn't really show or hurt until the damage is done. By the time your child complains or the skin looks red, it's too late.

• A baby or toddler is likely to be more sensitive to the sun than you are.

• Fair skinned children (and adults) are usually more sensitive than those with darker skin.

• Areas of skin that are rarely exposed to sun and air (the diaper area, for example) are more likely to burn than parts of the body that are not kept covered all the time. Remember this before you let your toddler romp around the yard or the beach without clothes.

• If you go to the beach or anywhere you will be spending a lot of time in the sun, keep your baby or toddler comfortably covered to prevent sunburn. Use a shirt with long sleeves, long pants, and a hat with a wide brim. A beach umbrella is a must if there's no natural shade available.

Should you use a sunscreen on your baby or toddler? A sunscreen cream, oil, or lotion may help, but it's best not to depend on one completely. Different products provide different levels of protection, and it's important to read the labels carefully. (The higher the rating number, the more protection provided.) Some young children might be sensitive to certain of the ingredients or the fragrances in some sunscreen preparations. It's best to ask your physician if you should use a sunscreen for your child and if so, which one you should use.

123

Treatment for Sunburn

Prevention is the best treatment for sunburn. If it's already too late for prevention, here are some suggestions.

• Apply cool water compresses several times a day to the most painful parts.

• Calamine lotion is soothing. Apply it generously.

• Vitamin E oil is expensive, but some people find it to be healing.

• Let your child soak in a cool Epsom-salts bath.

• Have the child wear very soft, loose fitting clothing to avoid creating further irritation.

• Stay out of the sun completely until your child's skin is healed.

If your child appears badly burned or seems to be very uncomfortable, consult your doctor. Call the doctor immediately if the child has nausea, chills or fever.

SWALLOWED OBJECTS

Mobile babies and toddlers tend to put things in the mouth, which is why small objects should be kept safely out of reach. No matter how careful you are, however, there may be an occasion when your child swallows something you wish he or she hadn't. Most swallowed objects—if they reach the stomach—will pass right on through the digestive system with no problem. (See Choking, page 41, for dealing with objects that are inhaled.)

If the swallowed object is something you wish to retrieve (a piece of jewelry or a coin, for example) or if it's something that might get stuck and cause harm (such as a pin) check the child's stools so you know when or if the object has been passed. To check the stools, wash them through a piece of screening or a sieve with warm or hot water. The screen will keep the object from going down the toilet or drain. If the missing object isn't passed within two or three days, or if the child seems to have discomfort, digestive upset, or bloody stools, call the doctor.

SWIMMING

In many localities there are swimming programs available for infants and toddlers. Should you enroll your child in such a program? If you think you really want to take your child to swimming class, try it and see how it goes. Many young children seem to enjoy these programs. (Make sure that the pool you're using has a warm enough water temperature and be careful that your child doesn't get chilled.)

If the idea of infant swimming classes doesn't appeal to you, don't bother. You haven't failed as a parent if your three-year-old still doesn't swim, although swimming is a pleasurable and useful skill which at some point should be included in your child's education.

Even if your baby or toddler does learn to swim, the acquisition of this skill does not eliminate (or even diminish) the need for supervision in water activities. An unattended baby could drown in the bathtub even if he or she knows how to swim. Swimming skill is no guarantee of safety for toddlers playing unsupervised on a riverbank or at poolside.

TALKING

Talking isn't something you must consciously teach to a child, and even if you wanted to you probably couldn't. Learning to talk has its own built-in timetable, and for most children speech develops at its own pace and in its own way. While there are no special talking lessons you could or should sit down to teach to your child, there are things you can do to facilitate his or her language learning.

Listening and comprehending are essential steps a child must take in learning to talk. One of the most valuable things you can do for your child is to give him or her lots of conversation to listen to. Providing a continuous example of conversation is far more useful than trying to teach the child to say certain words or phrases as you would train a parrot.

Provide opportunity for your child to develop an understanding of the meaning of words and phrases. Label things and point them out as you say what they are. Describe events as they are happening, so that the child can see the connection between words and what's going on.

Your child's language will develop best in a pleasant social context. If you are pleased with your child's early language efforts, he or she is likely to keep on trying. If, on the other hand, you keep correcting the child and try to insist that articulation be clear and syntax correct, you're likely to create more tension than talking. (See Baby-Talk, page 20. For specific suggestions and activities as your child learns to talk, see page 88.)

TANTRUMS

Temper tantrums are not uncommon among children between the ages of one and three, so don't be shocked or even surprised if your toddler has a tantrum from time to time. A tantrum is the way a toddler, who doesn't yet have all the language he or she needs to communicate, expresses anger and deals with frustration. Lying down kicking, screaming, and banging on the floor, or tearing about in an uncontrolled rage, is how a child trying to become independent may respond to being thwarted.

Some children, particularly bright and very active ones, may get a bit carried away with their efforts to achieve independence. They know what they want, and they become fiercely angry when they can't get it. Although tantrums are a normal toddler response to being frustrated, that doesn't mean you have to enjoy them or even encourage them as a means of self expression. It's best to deal with tantrums in a way that will minimize both their frequency and their ill effects.

Coping with a Tantrum.

The exact strategy you use for coping with your child's tantrums will, of course, depend on how your child reacts. Use what works best.

• Keep your child from getting hurt or from hurting anyone else. You may also need to protect things from your rampaging child. Either move the child, or move objects from his or her path.

• Some parents find that ignoring the tantrum works best. This is especially true if an audience seems to intensify your child's tantrum behavior. Make sure your child is safe, stay out of the way, and let the tantrum run its course.

• If you are unable or unwilling to ignore your child's tantrum, here's another approach. Hold the child gently on the floor. This will keep the child safe. Your presence, along with kind, gentle firmness, can be reassuring and comforting when the rage starts to diminish. This technique works for many children, but not all.

• A few children react even more violently to being touched during a tantrum. If your child is one of these, don't use force. If you fight back, everyone will lose. Clear the path, stay out of the way, and be ready to move in when the tantrum is over

• Don't bother trying to talk sense to a toddler who's in the middle of a tantrum. Reason and rage can't operate simultaneously.

• If the tantrum is happening in a public place (the playground, an aisle in the supermarket) it's probably best to remove the child from the situation so that you can deal with the tantrum in your own way.

• Don't reward the tantrum, but don't punish it either. The child should score no points for stopping a tantrum, but shouldn't lose any for having had one. When the tantrum is over, pick up exactly where you left off.

• As soon as the tantrum starts to subside, get on with whatever activity makes sense at that time. Try to get the child involved in doing something. A story, a nap, a walk outside, or a snack—it really doesn't matter as long as it's neither a reward nor a punishment for the tantrum. Whatever follows should be a quick return to normal routine.

Preventing Future Tantrums

• Don't give in to what caused the tantrum. For example, if it was a forbidden sweet your child wanted, don't produce one at the tantrum's end. If refusal to put on shoes was the tantrum trigger, don't yield and permit a barefoot afternoon. If a demand for a product you didn't want started a tantrum in the supermarket, don't buy the item just to keep the peace. If you give in, your child will quickly learn that you can be manipulated by his or her temper.

• Many children are more likely to have tantrums when very tired. If fatigue contributes to your child's tantrum behavior, try to prevent it. If an extra nap isn't possible, at least make an effort to avoid situations which are likely to add additional frustration to the child's tiredness.

• Other discomforts may also contribute to the likelihood of a tantrum. A comfortable child (not too warm or too cold, not hungry, not insecure) is less likely to have a tantrum.

• Try to divert your child from a situation which is likely to cause a tantrum. This doesn't mean you should give in to a child's whims. It does mean that you should be clever enough to present your demands in a way that won't set up a power play. For example, make a game out of getting dressed instead of demanding that your child sit still for the shoes.

• Be tactful and courteous to your child. No matter how tempted you might be, don't respond to a tantrum by descending to toddler emotional level. If you must make your child do something he or she doesn't want to do (and you will, for life is like that), be as nice about it as you can be. Leave your child a way to get out of impossible situations without losing face.

TEASING

Teasing your baby or toddler is not really an appropriate form of entertainment for either of you although it may seem harmless enough at the time. A young child is not an able match for an adult. Don't use teasing or ridicule as a form of discipline. Remember that a young child tends to take everything at face value. The literal-minded youngster may not be able to distinguish between a teasing remark and one that's intended to be carried out. In some cases this could cause unnecessary anxiety or unhappiness. Who knows what a child really thinks and feels when a parent says something like, "Do that again and I'll kill you." In dealing with a young child, it's best to say what you mean and mean what you say.

TEETHING

For some babies teething causes considerable discomfort and is accompanied by drooling, irritability, and a tendency to put objects of all sorts into the mouth. For others you'll hardly know it's happening until a click on the spoon tells you your child has his or her first tooth.

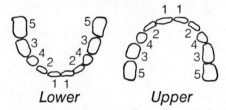

Lower   Upper

		Lower	Upper
(1)	central incisors	6-9 months	8-10 months
(2)	lateral incisors	11-14 months	9-12 months
(3)	first molars	18 months	18 months
(4)	cuspids	18-20 months	18-20 months
(5)	second molars	2-3 years	2-3 years

This diagram shows the usual order and approximate timing of the arrival of a child's baby teeth. Keep in mind, however, that these times may vary quite a bit from one child to another. A baby who gets teeth early is not necessarily bright or more advanced in other ways, nor is late teething an indication of backwardness.

The first teeth are generally cut with a minimum of distress. If it's just the first teeth your child is getting, problems such as digestive upset, diarrhea, or fever are probably not related to the teething, and may be a sign of other illness. If your baby seems sick, consult the doctor. Don't attribute the symptoms to teething and hope they will go away.

The first and second molars are likely to cause the most teething discomfort. Your child might be irritable, cranky or even miserable for some time while these teeth are coming in. Here are some suggestions to ease the discomforts of teething.

• Cold eases gum pain. Let your child have an ice cube wrapped in a handkerchief or tied into a clean baby's sock. Iced liquids feel good in the mouth. Try freezing juice in a paper cup until it's a bit mushy and let your child drink it or take it with a spoon.

• A hard rubber teething toy or ring for chewing on may provide some relief or at least some diversion from the discomfort.

• There's a type of teething ring filled with a gel which, if stored in the refrigerator between uses, can provide a nice cold chewing surface. If you do give your child one of these be careful that he or she doesn't use the teeth that are already there to bite through the ring's surface. Although the gel is said to be nontoxic, it should stay inside the teether and not end up inside your child.

• Massage the child's sore gums with your finger. This may help, and it indicates to your child that you understand about the hurting and that you care.

• A popular oldtime (and effective) remedy for teething pain is to rub a bit of brandy or whisky on the child's sore gums. If neither you nor your baby's doctor objects to this practice, try it.

• Don't administer pain relievers such as baby aspirin or fever drops unless your child's doctor specifically instructs you to do so. The doctor may suggest a topical pain reliever such as Oragel.

If your child seems to be in a lot of pain, check carefully to make sure that there isn't a different problem instead of or in addition to teething. For example, an obviously troubled child who keeps touching the side of the face may be suffering from an earache rather than new teeth. Don't be afraid to call your child's doctor for advice.

TELEVISION

Perhaps the most certain thing about television in today's world is that most children watch far too much of it. For children between the ages of two and eleven, an average child's viewing time exceeds 25 hours per week, which works out to more than 3½ hours daily. For preschool children these periods in front of the tube may represent a substantial portion of his or her waking hours.

What does the daily dose of television do to or for children? How can a parent use television wisely as entertainment and an educational tool without permitting it to be the dominant force in a child's life? Here are some things to consider.

Some TV Plusses

• Television can expose children to a wide variety of interesting people, places, and things which many children might never have the opportunity to experience in person.

• Television can increase a child's vocabulary by exposing the child to new words and their meanings.

• Some children's programming does teach useful skills or send appropriate messages to preschool children. Many youngsters do, for example, learn their letters and number concepts from *Sesame Street. Mr. Rogers' Neighborhood* provides valuable lessons and information in a calm, low key tone which you might find boring but a very young child is likely to find interesting as well as reassuring.

• Television does attract a child's attention, and the time an active toddler spends watching TV can give caregivers a chance to accomplish other essential tasks.

• If carefully chosen, television programs may provide suitable role models as well as interesting experiences for young children.

Some TV Minuses

• Television requires nothing of the child other than sitting in front of it. The child passively receives what the screen presents and need not respond actively in any way. This may lead to a tendency to process information superficially and may actually hinder a child's intellectual development.

• Television has a mesmerizing effect. The powerful and ever-changing images can be, for some children, overwhelming.

• Many television programs, from news broadcasts to entertainment shows, contain levels of violence that are undesirable for children's viewing. (See Violence, page 143.)

• Television advertising creates unnecessary and artificial demands for numerous products. This may, in turn, lead to family tensions as you are faced with teaching your toddler that it's impossible to have everything he or she sees and wants.

• The time a child spends watching television could often be better spent doing something else. For many children, TV consumes time that could otherwise be spent looking at books, playing with suitable toys, being outside in the fresh air, or interacting with other people.

• While television may add to a young child's list of known vocabulary words, it may also cut down on the personal interactions which are essential to the development of language as a tool for communication. Family members who spend a great deal of time in front of the TV set are likely to spend less time talking to each other.

• While television *can* provide suitable role models for children, it frequently does not. TV often presents unrealistic depictions of various occupations as well as sex role and minority group stereotypes.

Using Television Wisely

• Maintain complete control over your child's television viewing. Carefully monitor the content of the programs he or she watches and limit the total number of hours permitted. Make your own decisions about how much is too much, but keep in mind that less TV time is likely to be better. *You,* rather than your child, should be the custodian of the on/off switch, the channel selector, and the volume control.

• Talk about what your child has seen on television with him or her. Try to help your child do more than passively soak up what he or she sees. Encourage active responding and application of appropriate learnings to other activities.

• Don't leave the television on continuously. Turn it on for specific programs and then turn it off. Avoid having TV as the background noise for the rest of family life.

• Don't get into the habit of using TV regularly as an electronic baby-sitter, although there will be times when you will welcome the opportunity to keep your toddler engaged while you do something you must do. Try to keep these times few and far between if you can.

• Be sure that your child has lots of other things to do. A busy child doesn't need to sit in front of a television set.

TEMPERAMENT AND PERSONALITY

Personality is an individual's behavioral style. While some aspects of your child's developing personality may be influenced by the people and circumstances in his or her surroundings, much of a person's behavioral style seems to be inborn. Right from the start, a baby will show distinctive characteristics of temperament which strongly influence personality development. The behavioral pattern that a child demonstrates from birth is likely to persist. Try to understand and work *with* your child's behavioral style, because try as you will, you're unlikely to be able to change it.

Here are some areas of behavior in which babies seem to be born with temperamental differences.* These differences tend to remain as a baby grows into toddlerhood and beyond.

Activity
Some babies lie very still while being tended to, while others kick and wriggle about. Quiet babies tend to be tranquil toddlers, while the extremely active ones continue to have a high activity level.

Regularity
Some children seem to be born with a built-in timetable. They eat, sleep, and need to be changed at about the same times each day. A few children are completely unpredictable, and never seem to repeat the same schedule two days in a row. Most children are somewhere in between the two extremes.

Approach-Withdrawal, and Adaptability
Some children don't seem to mind new experiences at all, while others tend to withdraw and shrink away from them. Adaptable children get used to new things quickly, while nonadaptable children take much longer to adjust to changes.

Threshold of Responsiveness, and Intensity
Some children are more sensitive to stimuli than others. Some seem to notice the slightest suggestion of a noise or movement, while others may seem quite unaware of surrounding chaos. And, when they do respond, some children respond very vigorously, while others respond with far less intensity.

Persistence, and Distractibility
Some children cry continuously when they are hungry or in need of attention, and they don't stop demanding until they get what they need. Less persistent children make intermittent demands. Some children are very distractible and can be diverted from one thing to another, and can even be distracted from sucking at the breast or bottle. Others seem to be able to nurse or carry on with a task without taking notice of anything else.

Quality of Mood
Some children are generally in good humor. A few, however, seem to have been born with a perpetual cloud surrounding them, and nothing seems to suit them.

Children whose reponses tend to be moderate are generally easier to handle. Children who are slow to warm up—shy in approach and slow to adapt —can, with support and patience, adjust well to situations and function much like their more adaptable friends. Try not to become discouraged if your child is one of those whose temperament makes him or her hard to handle. Children who are especially sensitive, intense, nonadaptable or difficult to please may be harder to deal with, although such children may be especially exciting and rewarding once you get to understand them. If you understand that certain behaviors are part of a child's temperament, you will be better able to develop appropriate strategies for dealing with them.

*The material on which this section is based can be found in *Behavioral Individuality in Early Childhood,* by A. Thomas, S. Chess, H. Birch, et al. (New York University Press, New York: 1963).

TEMPERATURE (Environment)

Don't keep your child in overheated rooms or wrapped up in too many layers of clothing. Some conscientious parents mistakenly believe that it's necessary to keep a child's room especially warm. This is not so. Your baby or toddler will do very nicely at whatever temperature you normally keep your home. If you need a sweater to be comfortable, your child probably does too. But as a general rule, a child doesn't need more layers than you do, so don't put an extra sweater on the child just to be safe. Many parents overdress their children, and this practice is not a healthful one. Don't be misled by the temperature of your child's hands. A young child's hands normally feel cool, and if you keep putting on clothing in an effort to warm the child's hands, you will have a very warm child indeed. Use common sense and let your own comfort be a guide.

TEMPERATURE (Taking Child's)

There are two ways you can take your child's temperature — the rectal method and the axillary (armpit) method. Never put a thermometer in the mouth of a child under the age of five. Digital thermometer strips are not reliable and should not be used. Feeling the child's forehead will not give you an accurate indication if fever is present. The only way to be sure is to use a thermometer.
Here's how to take your child's temperature.

(1) Shake the thermometer down so that the mercury is well below the normal mark. This is easy to do. Just hold the thermometer at the high temperature end and snap your wrist sharply a few times. (Don't hold the thermometer over a table or other hard surface while you do this!)

(2) For the rectal method, lubricate the bulb of the thermometer with a dab of Vaseline. Hold the child face down on your lap and insert the thermometer about an inch into the rectum. If you meet resistance, start again. Do not force. Don't let go of the child or the thermometer at any time. If you are having trouble holding your child still, you can get a fairly accurate reading in about a minute, although 2–3 minutes are better.

(3) For the axillary method, simply place the thermometer in the child's armpit and hold the arm to the child's side. Wait at least four full minutes before reading the temperature.

The rectal method is slightly more accurate than the axillary method. Although some parents are a bit anxious at first, it's really not very difficult to take a child's rectal temperature and this method is actually easier and quicker.
One major advantage to the axillary method, however, is that you can use it when your child is asleep.
Make sure that you know how to read the thermometer correctly before you need to use it. If you are unsure about this, don't be afraid to ask. If you need to call your child's doctor, always report the exact temperature and the method you used to get it. (See also Fever, page 72.)

TERRIBLE TWOS

Before your toddler gets there, you'll probably hear numerous and dire warnings about the "terrible twos." Beware, however, of letting such talk turn into a self-fulfilling prophecy. While it's true that life with a two-year-old is likely to have its terrible moments, there can be lots of very pleasant times that no one will bother to comment on. People who point out how wonderful or exciting a two-year-old child can be are about as usual as newspaper headlines that proclaim good news. Nevertheless, there are many things about being two that can be terrific rather than terrible.

While the typical two-year-old may well provide you with contrariness, tantrums, dawding, or troublesome curiosity, he or she can also cause delight with responsiveness, love, language, and new accomplishments.

Make an effort to notice and enjoy all the good things, because some day not too far off you'll probably be wondering where all the time has gone and why it passed so fast.

(See also Contrariness, page 46; Dawdling, page 51; and Tantrums, page 125.)

THUMB SUCKING

Some children use sucking a thumb, finger, or fist to satisfy comfort needs or as a comfort device. Other children, if offered a pacifier, use that. Still others don't suck anything at all other than a bottle or the mother's breast for food.

If your child sucks his or her thumb, don't worry about it or make a fuss. The thumb is a safe, built-in, and portable pacifier that's always there when the child needs it and is completely under his or her control.

A thumb-sucking child sucks because the practice is pleasurable and comforting, and he or she will stop sucking when the need is no longer there. Trying to stop a child from sucking is usually counterproductive. The bigger deal you make of it, the more likely you are to prolong the practice. Parents who resort to bribes, threats, punishment, ridicule, or awful tasting substances are making much more of thumb sucking than it deserves. They risk creating additional tensions which only intensify the child's need to use sucking for comfort. Parents who provide a secure and loving environment, and leave the thumb sucking alone, are likely to find that the child's habit will diminish and simply disappear some day.

TOILET TRAINING AND TOILET LEARNING

Few childrearing topics engender as much talk, fuss, tension, and overthinking as toilet training. What can and should be just another step in a child's development often becomes a source of anxiety and failure for both parents and child.

You've probably already heard countless tales about how "Little So-and-So" was completely trained at less than a year. These stories are usually accompanied by the comment, "I see *your* child is still wearing diapers," said in a tone calculated to make you feel like a parenting failure. Pay these tormentors no mind. If the facts about these early toilet training success stories were known, you would quickly realize that in each case it was not the child who was trained, but the caregiver who simply managed more often than not to park the child's bottom over a potty just in time.

Toilet *training* is what the caregivers try to do. Toilet *learning* is the child's accomplishment, and true toilet learning can't occur until a child is able and willing. The child must recognize the need to go, hold the urine or movement until he or she is on the toilet or potty, and then release it. Most children are not ready—either physiologically or psychologically—to accomplish these steps until at least the middle of their second year. No amount of pressure can make readiness speed up.

Most children, regardless of when toilet training efforts are begun, are able to stay relatively dry and clean by the age of two-and-one-half to three years. Earlier starts at training do not usually lead to earlier successes, but they do drag the process out much longer and provide more opportunity for conflict.

Readiness for Toilet Learning

It's best to begin your child's toilet training when he or she is ready to learn. Readiness usually occurs some time between 18 and 30 months of age. Here are some signs that a child is ready.

• When he or she regularly wakes up dry in the morning or after a nap, and stays dry for two or more hours between diaper changes during the day, readiness is likely.

• The child ready to learn to use the toilet tells you when he or she is about to go. Before this, most children are able to tell you that they are in the process of going.

• The child who asks to be changed or who attempts to change his or her own diaper is ready to begin learning to use the toilet.

• A child who asks to use the toilet or shows some interest in the process is indicating readiness.

When your child shows these signs of readiness, it's time to begin teaching him or her how to use the toilet, but don't wait so long to be sure your child is ready that the period of optimum readiness passes by. If you don't teach your child when these signs of readiness are noted, he or she might lose interest in bothering with toilet learning, and training won't be nearly as easy as it might have been when enthusiasm and eagerness were ready to work for you.

Toilet Equipment

A small potty chair that the child can get on and off without help is best. A few children fear the height of a seat attached to an adult toilet, and some are frightened by the noise of a flushing toilet. Even if your child has no such fears, a toddler-size potty toilet is easier to manage. (Remove the deflector designed to keep a little boy's urine in the pot. A wet floor is preferable to an injured penis.) The sooner a little boy learns to urinate standing up, the better. The pot should be easy to remove and empty, and many children take pride in completing this final step of using the small toilet successfully.

Don't waste money on a potty chair which plays a tune or rings a bell when the urine or bowel movement is deposited in the bowl. The novelty of such an item quickly wears off, and may even distract the child from the task at hand. Many clever children quickly discover ways to activate the reward without urinating or having a bowel movement. A glass of milk or a small toy thrown into the pot does just as well as the intended products.

Toddlers usually find rolls of toilet tissue to be great fun. The roll will last longer if it's out of reach of the child's potty chair. Let your child take one handful of toilet tissue before sitting down. For bowel movements, a disposable wipe will be easier for the child to use. (Remember to teach a little girl to wipe from front to back, so that germs from the bowel movement are not introduced into the vagina.)

When Your Child Is Ready

When your child is ready, capitalize on the readiness and get on with the job of helping him or her to succeed at toilet learning. The best approach is to be easygoing and relaxed. When your child wakes up dry, the potty chair should be the next stop. Suggest using the potty whenever you think it's time. If the child doesn't want to, don't force. Be pleased at the successes and don't make a big fuss over the inevitable failures. Simply say, "Next time try to put the peepee (or whatever term you use) in the little toilet over there." If you make clear what the child is supposed to do, and provide encouragement and support, chances are the child will learn to use the toilet quite readily. If you make a big deal or a battle out of toilet training, you'll increase the likelihood of a long term problem.

> If the relaxed, easy going approach to toilet training appeals to you, an excellent resource is the little book *No More Diapers!*, by Joae Graham Brooks, M.D., and members of the staff of the Boston Children's Medical Center (Delacorte Press, New York: 1971). This appealingly illustrated paperback contains two stories about toilet learning — one for a girl and one for a boy— to read to a toddler. The introduction contains suggestions for parents or other caregivers on using the book to aid in teaching young children to use the toilet.

An Alternative Approach

If you think you would prefer more direction in toilet training your child, try reading *Toilet Training in Less Than a Day,* by Nathan H. Azrin and Richard M. Foxx, Ph.D. (Pocket Books, New York: 1974). This structured behavior modification approach to training your child to use the toilet is very effective if used as directed. It's best to read the book and decide if you'd like to use this technique before you've tried other methods. Don't be misled by the "less than a day" claim in the title. You still have to wait until your child is ready before using this technique, and many children continue to have accidents even after learning what they are to do. Nevertheless, the book can help you communicate to your child what is expected, and the step-by-step guidelines leave little to the imagination. If you do decide to try the approach outlined by Azrin and Foxx, consider using edible or tangible rewards other than candy to reinforce the desired toileting behavior. Candy will work, to be sure, but it's unwise to build the experience of sweets as snacks into your child's expectations. By doing this you may introduce a new problem, even though you accomplish the toilet training.

TONSILS

Tonsils are masses of lymphoid tissue on each side of the throat. Tonsils act as a filter to trap disease-causing germs. Years ago the tonsils, if enlarged, were routinely removed in an effort to prevent sore throats and upper respiratory problems. It is now recognized that the tonsils are an important part of the body's defense mechanism against infection. Most young children have enlarged tonsils. In a child, enlarged tonsils are not necessarily the sign of a problem but are more likely an indication that the tonsils are actively working at their job. Removal of the tonsils for a child under five is almost never recommended any more, because even tonsils scarred by infection are likely to have some capacity to perform their function.

If your child seems frequently to have a sore throat with swollen and sore tonsils, consult your pediatrician for advice. The doctor may do a throat culture and prescribe an antibiotic if the germs are bacterial in nature. You should try to make your child as comfortable as possible. Fluids, especially cold ones, may help. Extra humidity in a house with dry air may be helpful. (See Vaporizers, page 142.) Like common colds, these sore throats involving the tonsils are likely to become less frequent as your child gets older.

TOYS

Toys are a child's tools for learning as well as for entertainment. Young children learn by doing—touching, manipulating, and playing with things. While it's important to make toys available to your child, it's not necessary to spend a lot of money on them. In fact, your child may well learn more from and have more fun with everyday objects found around the house and yard than with elaborate or expensive purchased playthings. For example, the same toddler who rapidly tires of the costly doll which does everything—walk, talk, drink, wet, and wave "bye-bye"—may willingly spend hour after hour with a few pots, pans, and spoons creating lovely dirt and leaf dinners for you and imaginary playmates. Here are some guidelines for toy buying.

- Keep in mind that a toy labeled "educational" may not be. For a toddler, choose toys which encourage the child to be creative and imaginative. Avoid the complicated device which does the whole job and requires little input from the child. Such items quickly lose their appeal.

- Toys for a toddler should be sturdy, safe, and washable.

- In addition to the stores which you would expect to sell toys, try preschool supply outlets, mail order catalog companies, garage sales, and flea markets as sources for toys.

- Buy toys you want your child to have and will let him or her play with. If you can't stand noise, for example, don't buy a drum set and get angry every time it's used. Don't buy a wheeled riding toy if the only place it could be used is the living room where you won't permit it.

- Think of your child and his or her interests before you buy a particular toy. Is the toy suitable? Do you think your child will like it?

- If you wish to avoid creating stereotyped sex roles for your toddler, be sure to include some toys which traditionally have been associated with children of the opposite sex. For example, you could buy tools or a model sports car for a girl, and small cleaning implements or a doll for a boy.

TOY SAFETY

The recall of an unsafe toy may eventually remove it from the marketplace, but this often occurs after children have been injured or killed. You should judge for yourself whether or not a particular toy would be safe for your child. Use common sense along with the following guidelines suggested by the U.S. Consumer Product Safety Commission.

- Toys intended for older children should not be given to a toddler. What's safe for a third grader could be very dangerous for a two-year-old.

- Be alert for things which could be swallowed. Avoid tiny toys or toys which have parts which your child could remove.

- Don't let your toddler play with pointed objects such as knives, scissors, knitting needles, etc. Beware of seemingly safe toys which could be dismantled to reveal sharp features.

- Electrical toys which require plugging in are not safe for young children. Make sure that any battery operated toy is specifically designed for toddler use before turning your child loose with it.

- Toys which shoot things (darts, arrows, rockets, etc.) are never safe for young children. Even those with rubber "safety" tips could seriously damage a child's eye, and such tips can often be removed to create additional hazards.

- Avoid toys with sharp edges. Even if a toy doesn't start out with sharp edges, beware of those items which are fragile enough to be broken into sharp-edged pieces.

- Keep things with strings away from babies, and never let a toddler take a pull toy to bed.

- Toys such as cap pistols or guns which make extremely loud noises can damage a child's hearing as well as irritate caregivers and aid undesirable, violent play.

Do not store your child's toys in a toybox or trunk with a lid. Such storage containers have been known to trap young children and cause serious injury or even death. Open cardboard cartons covered with contact paper are a much better choice.

TRAVEL BY AIR

Traveling with a mobile baby or toddler isn't nearly as easy as toting a newborn aboard a plane or train, but it can be managed with a bit of careful planning. For long distance travel, flying is usually best if you can afford it. You'll get there faster and with the least effort. An infant (under two years of age) flies free on domestic flights and for ten percent of the accompanying adult's fare on international routes. Fares for a child age two or older vary with the airline. Here are some hints to make air travel with a baby or toddler as easy as possible.

Before You Go

- Make your reservations early. A good travel agent doesn't cost extra, and using one is far easier than calling airlines and trying to figure out the best fares and flights on your own.

- A travel agent will help you request the most suitable seats on the plane for travel with a child. On a jumbo jet, seats by the doors have the most legroom —more than enough for you to stretch out completely and arrange your child comfortably en route. (Doors must be clear for takeoff and landing, but in the air the space is yours.) Avoid bulkhead seats in the center, where there might be a movie going on right over your head and a line of people in the aisle on the way to the restrooms. On standard size planes, seats by a bulkhead or an emergency exit usually have the most legroom.

- Don't forget to take your child's car restraint along with you. You'll need it to keep your child safe in a car when you get to your destination. (This may not be necessary if you plan to rent a car and you have reserved a child restraint in advance.) The seat can be checked with your luggage. It's crash proof, and it doesn't need to be boxed. Just make sure it has a tag on it with your name and address.

• Pack an easy-to-open, lightweight flight bag with everything you think you'll need en route and then a few extras just in case. You'll need bottles for an unweaned baby if you're not breast-feeding. Take one bottle of water if you are breast-feeding. You'll need baby food if your child is on solids but not ready for an airline meal. Bring a generous supply of disposable diapers and disposable wipes. Many airlines have these on board, but don't take the risk of being without. One complete change of clothes is a wise precaution.

At the Airport and On the Plane

• Ask your travel agent or the airline how early you should check in for your flight. Remember that getting anywhere with a small child is likely to take longer than it should, but don't leave so much time that you have to endure what may seem like a never-ending wait.

• On a full flight, your child must sit on your lap or be on the floor at your feet if he or she is under two and has not paid for a seat. If the plane is not full, most airlines will try to place you next to an empty seat so your child needn't spend the entire flight on your lap. Remember that this is a courtesy, however, and you are not entitled to it. So ask nicely.

• Bring a bag of things to keep your child entertained. Small toys and games, crayons and a coloring book, and similar items should be included. If you gift-wrap a series of small "surprises," you can use these to help pass the time and to reward the child for good behavior. Plan a surprise for every twenty to thirty minutes or so, and tell the child that the next one can be opened if he or she plays nicely with the last one for that time. If you wrap the surprise cleverly, the unwrapping can consume a lot of time. Some of the surprises might be appropriate "munchies" such as crackers or a bit of fruit, or a sandwich.

• Let your child suck during takeoff and landing. The swallowing will help keep the ears comfortable as the pressure changes. (That's what the bottle of water is for, in case you prefer not to breast-feed at this time.) For an older child who has outgrown bottles, this is one time you ought to make an exception and permit gum chewing or sucking on a sweet.

• If you've paid for a seat for a toddler or older child, find out what the special child's menu is before you accept it in place of the regular airline meal. A sodium-laden hot dog or leathery hamburger might not be as wise a choice as the chicken everyone else is getting. For a baby still on formula, carry at least a two-day supply with you, especially on international flights. This will see you through in case your luggage temporarily goes astray

• No matter how tempted you might be to get an active child out of your hair for a few minutes, it's unwise to let a mobile baby crawl in the aisle or permit a toddler to wander about during the flight. Even a slight bit of turbulence could cause a mishap. And, no matter how cute and irresistible your child might be, it's not fair to let a small person bother other passengers who may or may not find these antics entertaining. Be courteous and thoughtful, and keep your child under your control at all times even though it may not be easy.

• Most flight attendants will go out of their way to make you and your child comfortable. However, they do have a job to do. The safety and comfort of *all* the passengers is their concern. They are not baby-sitters.

TRAVEL BY BUS

Although usually the least expensive, bus travel for a long distance is the hardest on you and your child. Avoid it if you can. If you can't, keep these points in mind.

• Bring everything you'll need for your child. Pack it in a small bag that's easy to handle. Particularly if the bus is crowded, you'll not have any room to maneuver.

• Be prepared to keep your baby on your lap for the entire trip unless you have paid for two seats. On a bus, there's really nowhere you can go.

• Practice changing your child right on your lap. A bus lavatory is very small and usually unsuitable for tending to an infant or toddler.

• Take courage from the fact that the droning noise of the bus may help keep your child sleeping for some of the time.

• For a mobile baby or toddler, pack a surprise bag just as you would for train or plane travel. Make sure that the items you include are small enough to be played with in a very confined area, because that's all the space you'll have.

• If your child is inclined toward motion sickness, the bus is probably a poor choice of transportation. Ask your child's physician for advice on medication for motion sickness prevention. Make sure you have a travel sickness bag handy in case the prevention doesn't work. (See Motion Sickness, page 95.)

TRAVEL BY CAR

The major advantage to long distance travel by car is that it's under your control. You can stop when you wish, or go on a little longer if the trip is going well. If you've forgotten something you need for your child, you can stop somewhere along the way and try to purchase a replacement. To keep your toddler happily occupied in the car, a bag of gift-wrapped surprises as suggested for planes, trains, or busses will work in a car as well. Be sure your child is correctly fastened into an approved car restraint whenever the car is moving. (See Automobile Safety, page 15.) If your child is inclined to get carsick, follow the suggestions under Motion Sickness, page 95.

If you're planning to stay in a motel or hotel with your toddler en route, it's preferable to make reservations in advance. This will give you a chance to select the most suitable facilities for traveling with a small child. Be sure to request a crib in advance if you're going to need one.

TRAVEL BY TRAIN

Long-distance train traval can be manageable with an infant or toddler as long as you plan ahead and pack carefully. Some families do enjoy train travel which does have the advantage of something to see out the window besides clouds. A long trip on a train with an active youngster can be very wearying.

• Bring everything you will need to care for your child en route. You will not be able to purchase any babycare items once you're underway. If you have a lot of luggage with you, pack the things you'll need for diaper changes and feedings in a small bag that's easy to manage with one hand.

• Try to keep your luggage to what you can manage without additional help. Porters are rarely available when you need them.

• Find seats in a car where smoking is not permitted.

• An umbrella stroller will enable you to walk your child up and down the aisle. The restrooms designed for the handicapped (identified by a wheelchair symbol) are spacious enough for you to wheel the stroller in with you.

• A bag of surprises (as suggested for air travel) to keep your child entertained is helpful. Wrap the items so that the unwrapping will take a long time. Include small toys and games, and appropriate snacks.

• Even if you regularly use cloth diapers, disposables are a must for traveling. Simply wrap up the used ones and toss them into the trash receptacles available in each train car.

• Don't count on the train serving food appropriate for your toddler. Bring what you need and have a "picnic."

• As on a plane, letting your mobile baby or toddler loose in the aisle of a train can cause an accident. Keep your child within your sight and under your control at all times.

TWINS

If you have twins (or triplets) you'll find that much of the information in this book pertains to your situation too. Many of the ingredients of good parenting do not vary with the number of children.

However, parents of multiples do need to develop special strategies for coping with more than one baby or toddler at the same time. There will be great joys and many interesting and exciting moments with your children. There will also be a lot more work. Don't get discouraged; it gets easier as your children get a bit older. The first few months are the toughest. Older baby and toddler twins are excellent companions for each other and some parents report that two are easier than one at that stage. Separation at bedtime may be less of a potential problem because twins will always have each other at this time.

> An excellent source of information and support for parents of multiples is a **Mother/Parents of Twins Club (MOTC)**. To find one in your area, check your local telephone book or ask your doctor. You can also write to **The National Organization of Mothers of Twins Clubs, Inc., 5402 Amberwood Lane, Rockville, MD 29853**. Many of the clubs have produced pamphlets, cassettes, and other helpful aids. Information about these can be obtained from the National Organization.

UNDERWEIGHT CHILDREN

If you make appropriate foods available to your baby or toddler, chances are he or she will eat what's necessary as long as you don't make a big deal about mealtime and attempt to force specific foods on a reluctant eater. Young children have strong survival instincts and won't deliberately starve themselves.

What should you do if you think your child's weight is not increasing at a rate to keep up with his or her height? Consult a physician before attempting to make changes in your child's diet. A lean build may well be natural for your child, in which case you should leave well enough alone. Gone are the days when plumpness in a young child was considered a sign of good health and caring parents. Chances are, if the child's lack of weight gain is caused by illness, there will be other symptoms. In any case, you should get medical advice if you are concerned.

VAPORIZERS

Overheated dry air can be irritating to the mucous membranes of the nose and throat and perhaps make children more vulnerable to the cold virus. Using a vaporizer or humidifier to add moisture to the air can help provide a healthier environment and make a person with a cold or breathing distress more comfortable.

For a mobile baby or toddler, it's safer to use a cold-mist humidifier rather than a steam vaporizer. If tipped over, a steam vaporizer could cause serious scalding. If your toddler can climb out of the crib, don't count on him or her—even if sick—to stay away from the steam. A cold-mist humidifier puts moisture into the air without the potential hazard. Pans of water on the radiator, or boiling kettles and pots will not provide enough moisture to make a real difference, and you don't want containers of boiling water near your toddler. So, if your child tends to have colds or other respiratory problems, invest in a cold-mist humidifier. You can probably get one in your pharmacy or hardware store.

VIOLENCE

Violence is far too much with us in this world, and we should make every effort to protect our children from exposure to violence wherever we may find it —in personal interactions, toys, or on television.

While you may find it impossible to eliminate entirely the examples of violence from your child's environment, you can take steps to teach your toddler that violent behavior and unbridled aggression are not acceptable.

Because there is a definite relationship between viewing violence on television and the aggressive behavior of children, you should monitor your toddler's television fare very closely to eliminate those shows in which violence abounds. Don't assume that a show is acceptable simply because it is aimed at a kiddie audience on Saturday morning. Certain children's cartoons may be among the worst offenders, and many toddlers are unable to differentiate between the actions they see on the screen and clobbering a playmate in real life.

Toys of violence do not belong in a young child's collection. Research has suggested that for many children, playing with toy guns significantly increases antisocial and aggressive behavior, and the typical toddler has no need for such stimulation. Although many children will point their fingers and say "Bang, bang!" or fashion their own "guns" out of sticks, this is not quite the same as using an object that is designed to resemble a real weapon. Let your child indulge in fantasy gunplay if you wish, but don't give it your overt approval and encouragement by providing the props. Guns are intended to maim and kill, and their use is not a lesson your toddler needs to practice.

A war toy designed with outer space or science fiction in mind is still a tool of violence and is unsuitable for a toddler. Zapping someone with a ray gun in another galaxy isn't any more civilized than machine gunning the natives in a jungle war or toppling someone off a horse with a six-shooter. Space wars are simply violence with a modern technological twist.

The best way to discourage violent play by your child is to keep toy weapons away from him or her without making a big deal out of it. Remember that a child under three is too young to comprehend lengthy explanations, so skip the lectures and make sure your child has lots of other things to do. When your child is old enough to draw a firm line between fantasy and reality, you may choose to permit certain toys that were unsuitable for a toddler unable to make such distinctions.

VISION (Problems)

If you suspect that your baby or toddler may have vision problems, discuss your observations and suspicions with your child's pediatrician. It's important to identify any difficulties as soon as possible so that efforts can be made to correct them. The pediatrician may refer your child to an eye specialist (ophthalmologist) for further testing.

Here are some questions to ask yourself as you observe your child.

• When you look at your child's eyes, do they appear to be working together? Or does one or both turn in or out and stay that way for any period of time? If one or both eyes seem to wander in any child three months or older report this to the doctor.

• Does your baby or toddler seem to be visually responsive? Does he or she look at things and make some eye movements that suggest that the things are being seen? If not, mention this to the doctor

• Does your mobile baby or toddler frequently bump into large objects or pieces of furniture while moving about? If so, ask your pediatrician to help you find out why.

• Does your child hold objects very close to look at them? When he or she tries to pick up a small object does the hand often miss the object? Does there seem to be a lack of coordination between eyes and hand movements? These behaviors suggest a possible vision problem.

• Does your child regularly appear to favor one eye over the other when looking at something? Does he or she frequently rub the eyes? Does your child blink, squint, or frown excessively? Does he or she often close one eye? Any of these symptoms should be mentioned to your pediatrician.

VITAMIN SUPPLEMENTS

It is possible to meet the vitamin needs of your older baby or toddler through a balanced diet. This means not only planning the meals and preparing them carefully to avoid excessive vitamin loss during cooking, but also getting the various foods inside the child on a fairly regular basis. It's that last step that may cause a problem, and it's best not to make mealtime a battleground.

Many families (and their physicians) feel that a vitamin supplement is an added safeguard to ensure that your child gets the necessary vitamins even on days when he or she is exercising toddler individuality about what to eat.

• Use liquid vitamins for a baby or for a toddler who can't or won't deal with tablets. The best way to administer them is to drop the prescribed dose right on the child's tongue using the measuring dropper provided. Many children like the taste. If that doesn't work, mix the drops in a very small amount (so you know the child will finish) of juice.

• If you plan to use chewable vitamins for your toddler or older child, choose and purchase them carefully. Most children's chewable vitamins contain large quantities of sugar, and these products may do as good a job creating work for your dentist as they do to prevent vitamin deficiencies in your child's diet. Many children's vitamin products contain ingredients that may be linked to hyperactivity or other behavioral problems. Avoid products with artificial coloring, artificial flavorings, and unnecessary preservatives, as well as excessive sweeteners. You'll do better if you buy vitamins without these extras and mash up a tablet into a spoonful of fruit to get it into your child.

• Never refer to vitamins (or any other tablet) as "candy," even though such a label wouldn't be far off as a description of the contents of many children's vitamin products. Children who think vitamins are candy might be tempted to help themselves when you're not looking, and this could be dangerous. Vitamins should have a childproof cap. Keep the container out of reach even if it does.

• Even if you take megadoses of vitamins and believe this practice to be helpful, it's unwise to dose your child in this way. Children are more susceptible to harm from a vitamin overdose, and there's no evidence that large doses of vitamins have any specific benefits for a child. Stick to a normal daily dose recommended by your child's pediatrician.

VOMITING

There are a number of possible causes of vomiting in a young child—illness such as a viral infection of the stomach, fright or upset, pain, injury, or an overdose of dinner. If your usually healthy child vomits after eating too much at a birthday party, chalk it up to an excess of goodies and excitement. Clean up the mess and give the child a little while to recover. If, however, your child vomits and you can't trace the cause to something relatively harmless, here are some questions to consider:

(1) Does the child appear sick? Is he or she acting strange?

(2) Is there fever? If so, how much?

(3) Is the vomiting accompanied by diarrhea?

(4) Is the child vomiting with great force (projectile vomiting) rather than simply throwing up?

(5) Does the vomiting persist? Has the child thrown up more than twice in a day?

(6) Does the child seem dehydrated? Is there a lack of saliva or tears? Is he or she passing less urine than usual?

(7) Does the child seem to have stomach pain? (It's often tough to be sure with a child who's too young to explain just where it hurts.)

(8) Has the child fallen on the head? Is he or she pale or drowsy?

If the answer to one or more of the above questions is "Yes," then it's best to call the child's pediatrician. The problem may just be a stomach virus that will run its course with no lasting harm. However, the vomiting could be a symptom of a more serious problem, and the sooner you find out what to do the better.

Treatment

If the cause of the vomiting is a mild stomach virus or a case of too much to eat, here are some suggestions to follow. (Of course, if you have contacted the child's doctor, you should follow specifically any directions given to you at that time.)

• Give the child's stomach a chance to rest. (It's unlikely that he or she will want to eat or drink anything anyway, but make sure that food is not available for a while.)

• If there has been no vomiting for two or three hours, you can try to start replacing the fluids which have been lost. Offer a small quantity (begin with a teaspoonful) of clear liquid such as water, juice, or ginger ale or cola that's gone flat. If the child can keep this down for ten minutes, give a little more. Continue to supply small quantities of liquid as long as the child can keep it down. The key to this treatment is to give small quantities at frequent intervals and not to overload the system with too much at once.

• A day of liquids can be followed by a day of light foods such as dry toast, cereal without milk, Jello, rice, apple sauce or bananas. Avoid milk, meat, or eggs for another day or two.

• If the child handles the light foods well, ease gradually back to a normal diet. Don't do it all in one meal.

WALKERS

A "walker"—a wheeled device which suspends a baby in an upright position, feet touching the floor—can make a prewalking baby very mobile indeed.

A walker isn't necessary to teach a child to walk, although many children have fun getting around in one. A walker is not a confinement device like a playpen to keep a child out of trouble. In fact, a walker may transport the child to potential trouble faster and even cause a few problems on its own. One recently published study reported that about half of the subjects studied had suffered some sort of injury while in a walker. While most of the problems were minor and required little or no further attention, some were severe enough to require hospitalization.

If you do decide to use a walker to make your mobile baby even more mobile, here are some safety hints.

• Don't leave your child unsupervised in a walker. The device is not a baby-sitter. Minor cuts, bruises, and pinched fingers are not uncommon side effects of walker use.

• Gates in front of stairs and steps are a must if your child is loose in a walker. A child who catapults down a flight of stairs in a walker could be seriously injured—perhaps even more seriously than he or she might have been hurt if he had tried to walk down the stairs and had tumbled.

• When the wheels of a walker meet the edge of a carpet, a doorstop, or other impediment to forward motion, the walker and the child might tip over

Most walker accidents are not serious, and nearly all of them could be prevented with close supervision. So, if you do permit your child to use a walker, it's important to pay attention and not depend on the device to keep your child safe.

WALKING

While most babies walk on their own by the age of 15 months or so, some who are perfectly normal take a while longer to get started. Some babies manage to take their first steps without any assistance at all, but many benefit from parental encouragement and support. While you shouldn't pressure your child to walk, it's fine to be helpful when he or she is ready to take that first step.

Before walking without holding onto anything, most children "cruise" for a while. This involves moving in a more or less standing position while holding onto something—a piece of furniture or the side of the crib or playpen—for support. When your child is standing well and seems ready to take a step or two without holding on, you can help. Sit on the floor just about within reach of where your child is standing. Hold out your arms and encourage the child to take that first step. Be patient, and one of those times the step will occur.

WATER (To Drink)

Offer water to your baby or toddler at least twice a day, more often in hot weather. Use a bottle if the child is not yet weaned—a cup or a glass (plastic is safest) if he or she can handle it. Many toddlers enjoy using a straw.

Sometimes a baby who seems to be demanding a feeding really isn't hungry, but thirst is the problem. Offer water, and if your child is thirsty he or she will probably drink it. If the need isn't there, the offer has caused no bother. Water is a much better choice for a thirsty child than sodas or fruit drinks which contain sweeteners and artificial colorings. If your child is extremely thirsty, water is even a better choice than milk which fills and adds calories without really quenching thirst. If early on you get your child used to taking a glass of water when thirsty, you will be building in a healthful habit for later years.

WEANING (From the Bottle)

You can wean your child from the bottle completely and relatively abruptly at a time of your choosing. Or you can let the child gradually wean himself or herself as he or she wishes. There are advantages and disadvantages to each approach.

Weaning at the Child's Pace

• The child gets comfort and pleasure as well as nourishment from sucking, and having the bottle available places this under the child's control. Use of a bottle may diminish the need for thumb sucking as a comfort device.

- An evening bottle feeding often makes relaxing before bedtime easier.

- Using a bottle helps ensure that the child will get enough milk.

- A gradual transition from bottle to no bottle is less likely to cause upset than abrupt weaning.

Weaning at a Definite Time

- A child may become increasingly attached to and dependent on his or her bottle as time goes on. If left to his or her own devices, the bottle might never be given up with complete willingness.

- Evening bottles which end up being taken to bed increase the chances of tooth decay.

- Children who drink bottles well into the second year may consume more milk than they need which, in turn, can lead to overweight.

- Once a mobile child discovers that a bottle is portable, the bottle takes on a new attractiveness and the child independently carts it about. Early weaning can eliminate the opportunity for this discovery.

Consider the pros and cons of definite weaning and choose whichever approach you think will work best for your child and your family's lifestyle. If you wish to be relaxed about weaning and let your child use the bottle as a comfort device as long as he or she wishes, there's no harm in it. If, on the other hand, you prefer to eliminate the bother of bottles and get your child completely to the cup as fast as feasible, that's fine too. Keep in mind, however, that your child may turn to other comfort devices when the bottle is no longer available.

Drinking From a Cup

Whether you wean your child completely at a particular time, or let nature take its course over weeks or months, you'll still have to teach your child how to drink from a cup. Here are some suggestions.

- A lightweight plastic cup is safest. A cup with two handles is easier to manage.

- Begin by putting just a swallow or two of milk in the bottom of the cup. This prevents the child from taking too much at once, and leaves less for the inevitable spill.

- You'll have to help your child hold and maneuver the cup at first until he or she figures out what to do with it. Guide his or her hand gently to get started.

- Some children find using a straw to be an excellent transition from sucking a bottle to sipping from a cup. Other children, however, don't seem to have a clue about how a straw works. You can try a straw to see if your child takes to it. The short straws which bend are best.

- If right from the start you give juice and water only from a cup and never put either of these drinks in a bottle, this will give your child a headstart on the weaning process.

• If you hold your child during bottle-feeding and *never* let him or her carry the bottle about, chances are that complete weaning will happen much more rapidly. If, on the other hand, your child learns to bring the bottle with him or her, chances are the bottle use will persist. Whichever approach you permit is up to you.

Training Cups

A training cup is a plastic cup with a lid and little spout with holes in it. Its purpose is to help prevent spills while easing the transition from bottle or breast to cup. Some children use the device effectively. Others, however, discover quite quickly that turning the cup upside down results in lovely little streams of milk pouring out. Try a training cup if you think it will help. If it doesn't work as intended for your child, discard the lid, and use it later as a regular cup.

WEANING (From the Breast)

Weaning from the breast is done best for both mother and child if it is done gradually. Depending on when you wean your breastfed child and how long you intend the process to take, you can either switch the baby to a bottle or directly to taking milk from a cup. For a child under six months old, you'll probably want to use bottles as an intermediate step. For a child who's already taking solid foods from a spoon and juice or water from a cup, you may wish to skip the bottle stage entirely. If you omit bottles, you'll probably have to stop nursing more gradually in order to meet your child's continuing sucking needs until they naturally diminish. You know yourself and your child, and you should do what you think is best.

To begin weaning your child from the breast, begin by giving up one feeding during the day. Most mothers find the midday feeding the easiest one to give up. Substitute milk in a bottle or cup, according to your plan, for the breast milk. If your child is already taking solid foods, give a little milk before the solid part of the meal and the rest of the milk afterwards. After you've stopped giving a regular feeding from the breast, your milk supply will naturally decrease. If your breasts are uncomfortably full, express a little milk to ease the discomfort, but not enough to stimulate additional milk production.

When you have successfully eliminated one daily feeding for two or three weeks, and you and your child have adjusted to the new schedule, eliminate another feeding. Whether you retain the evening feeding at the breast, or keep nursing at breakfast time is up to you. Many mothers find that keeping on with the evening feeding helps to relax a child at bedtime, but you should give up whichever feeding you think you and your child will miss the least. After you have reduced your nursing schedule to once daily, this feeding too will diminish and disappear completely.

As your child nurses less, your breasts will produce less and less milk until the child is completely weaned. There's no one right way to wean a child from the breast. Follow your instincts and do what works comfortably for both of you.

WELL BABY CLINICS

In some localities, a "well baby clinic" would be an economical alternative to using the services of a pediatrician in private practice. Routine checkups and immunizations can be attended to in this way. The availability of these facilities varies greatly from one area to another. Your local hospital or health department can probably provide information on what healthcare resources you can find for your child.

WORKING PARENTS

It is a reality in the 1980s that in many families with small children, both parents work outside the home. If this is the case in your family, or if you are a single parent who works, here are a few suggestions.

• Don't waste time or energy feeling guilty about the fact that work keeps you away from your child during a good part of the time. Put that effort into making the time you *do* have with your child as beneficial for both of you as possible.

• Don't apologize to your child for your job. Try to make it just another part of life in your family.

• Make childcare arrangements that you feel comfortable about. (See pages 19 and 52.) If you are not happy with the care your child is getting in your absence, you will worry at work and perhaps overcompensate at home. Both your working life and your home life will suffer along with your child's wellbeing.

• Face the fact that you may be very tired at the end of a day. (So are many parents who spend all day with an active toddler.) Try to plan time to do things with your child. No matter how exhausted you may feel, try not to skip some quiet play together or the bedtime story and other sleepy-time rituals.

• Your child's preschool years will pass by very quickly. You'll probably wake up one morning and wonder where they have gone. So, no matter what else you have to do, it's important to try and miss as little as possible during this time. Make the most of the precious little time you do have. (See pages 3-5 and 88-92.)

X-RAYS

If your child requires an X-ray, try to remain with him or her if at all possible. The procedure can be quite frightening. Explain that an X-ray is just a picture of part of the body taken with a special camera. Preparation in advance is helpful, but of course, if the reason for the X-ray is an emergency, you won't have that luxury. Most medical facilities will permit you to remain with your child during emergency treatment if at all possible. Indicate firmly your desire to stay with your child.

Avoid routine X-rays that are not essential for diagnosis of a problem. A lead shield should be used to protect your child's genitals when another body part needs an X-ray. Be sure to call this to the technician's attention.

ZINC OXIDE OINTMENT

Zinc oxide ointment (available in tubes or jars) is an effective and inexpensive treatment for diaper rash. Zinc oxide is a major ingredient in some of the brand-name diaper rash remedies such as Desitin.

ZOOS

Visiting a zoo can be an exciting learning experience for a toddler. However, remember that wild animals, even in captivity, are still wild animals. Keep your child under control at all times. Don't let any member of your family climb over guard rails for a closeup picture, no matter how tempted you might be. Hold on tightly to your child as he or she tosses peanuts to the elephants. In the children's section of the zoo, where children and tame animals are allowed to mingle, remember that your toddler's good judgment probably does not equal his or her curiosity. An afternoon at the zoo can be fun as long as you keep it safe and recognize your toddler's limitations. Be sure to bring an umbrella stroller, because your child will probably get tired of walking long before he or she tires of looking.

INDEX